TIME
SPECIAL EDITION

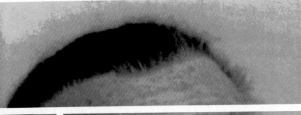

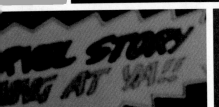

THE WORLD OF MARVEL

Stan Lee, Marvel kingpin, in 1991

The Spider-Man balloon (seen here in 2014) is always one of the most popular parts of the Macy's Thanksgiving Day Parade in New York.

CONTENTS

Parts of this edition were published previously by TIME.

WHY WE WORSHIP THESE HEROES

MARVEL'S ICONS THRILL US WITH THEIR SENSATIONAL EXPLOITS WHILE SIMULTANEOUSLY FORGING AN EMOTIONAL CONNECTION TO THEIR HUMANITY

BY RICH SANDS

FIVE OF THE TOP 11 HIGHEST-GROSSING FILMS of 2018 featured characters that originated on the pages of Marvel Comics. That's a remarkable legacy for a company that first began publishing 80 years ago. Back in 1939, Timely Comics (as it was then known) quietly churned out a variety of titles that were considered throwaway, lowbrow entertainment. It would be a few decades until Marvel, the so-called House of Ideas, revolutionized the comic-book genre, and another few decades before it did the same for pop culture as a whole.

"AND SO WAS born the Fantastic Four!!" read a panel in the first issue of a comic book that made its debut in the summer of 1961. "And from that moment on, the world would never again be the

same!!" The line, written by Stan Lee, specifically referred to the new superhero team he'd created with Jack Kirby. But in fact the statement applied to the entire world of comic books. *The Fantastic Four* No. 1 was a pioneering piece of literature— yes, even a comic book can be considered literature—and its realistic portrayal of heroes as complicated human beings transformed a genre that had long been derided as unsophisticated, stirring something in the young (and not-so-young) readers of the form. "Look at it this way. There were many, many super heroes merrily cavorting in their colorful little long johns before the FF made the scene," Lee wrote in his introduction to the 1987 collected edition *Marvel Masterworks Vol. 1.* "But virtually none of them had personal problems, none had to worry about earning a living,

The first issue of *The Fantastic Four* in 1961 (with vibrant art by Jack Kirby) introduced readers to Mister Fantastic, Invisible Girl, the Thing and a new version of the Human Torch (a character created in 1939). Though writer Stan Lee had no idea the series would catch on, "for just this once," he wrote years later, "I would do the type of story I myself would enjoy reading if I were a comic-book reader."

Chris Evans celebrated with fans at the 2015 premiere of Avengers: Age of Ultron.

none ever argued or lost their tempers with other super heroes. Not until our captivating little quartet came along."

As reader mail flowed into their New York City office, Lee and Kirby and their cohort (not to mention their bosses) realized they'd struck a chord. They continued to churn out more and more of their gallant-yet-still-relatable superheroes, including the Hulk, Spider-Man, Thor, the X-Men, the Avengers and hundreds of other charismatic characters. Soon the company was rechristened "Marvel" to fit with the spectacle of their exploits.

BY THE LATE 1970s, *The Uncanny X-Men* became Marvel's most popular comic-book series, thanks to daring story lines that paralleled real-life civil rights issues and appealed to many readers' feelings of being outsiders. The mutant characters were "feared and hated by the world they have

sworn to protect . . . the strangest heroes of all," as they were famously billed during writer Chris Claremont and artist John Byrne's memorable run on the comic. The X-Men faced discrimination that mirrored the racism, anti-Semitism and homophobia that pervaded (and still too often pervade) society. But these stories were more than just morality plays. A thrilling mix of science-fiction adventure and soapy drama among the characters was woven through a complex and constantly evolving narrative.

And it wasn't just rousing storytelling that drew a devoted following to Marvel. Lee was an inveterate showman, and he used the letters pages in the comics to interact with the fans, with whom he cultivated a chummy rapport. "Face front, True Believers!" was his call to attention, one of many signature catchphrases he coined over the years. "I wanted our readers to feel they're part of a group, an inner circle, and we're all having a lot of fun that the rest of the world doesn't know about," he recalled in the 2010 documentary *With Great Power: The Stan Lee Story*. Among his innovations were the creations of the Merry Marvel Marching Society fan club (which became as popular on college campuses as it was in elementary schools) and "Stan's Soapbox," a feature in which he addressed the controversial issues that were being tackled in the comics. "It seems to me," he wrote in one, "that a story without a message, however subliminal, is like a man without a soul. In fact, even the most escapist literature of all—old-time fairy tales and heroic legends—contained moral and philosophical points of view."

DECADES LATER, MARVEL'S multitudinous colorful characters have not only endured but thrived and dominated far beyond the pages of comic books. Who, in the 1960s—or even the early 2000s, for that matter—would have guessed that characters such as Iron Man, Ant-Man and a snarky talking raccoon called Rocket would become bona fide household names? Marvel amplified its reputation by taking chances on heroes (and villains) whose personalities, courage, flaws, humor and pathos allow us to relate, even if their specific situations involve battling alien warlords, traveling to mythological kingdoms or teaming up with a sentient, monosyllabic tree.

Love for these characters—be it on the page or onscreen or in video games—has been magnified by the growth of unabashed fan culture. Comic conventions across the country (and around the world) have brought geekdom out of the shadows. The Merry Marvel Marching Society may have disbanded long ago, but modern enthusiasts continue to flock to these events to meet the stars and creators, intensely debate plot points (Is Star-Lord to blame for undermining a plan to stop Thanos's decimation of half of humanity in *Avengers: Infinity War*?!) and, of course, show off their elaborate costumes based on their favorites. Respect must be paid to anyone willing to wear Loki's enormous horned headpiece or Captain Marvel's full-body spandex suit in the summer heat of San Diego.

> *Love for Marvel's characters—be it on the page or onscreen or in video games—has been magnified by the growth of unabashed fan culture.*

As the Marvel Cinematic Universe (MCU) continues to expand, so does the fan base. The astronomical success of the 2018 film *Black Panther*—the studio's highest-grossing domestic movie to date—highlighted the cultural impact of Marvel's properties. "Rather than dodge complicated themes about race and identity, the film grapples head-on with the issues affecting modern-day black life," Jamil Smith wrote in TIME on the eve of the release of the movie, which featured an African hero and a largely black cast and creative team. "It is also incredibly entertaining, filled with timely comedy, sharply choreographed action and gorgeously lit people of all colors."

And now Marvel Studios is about to release *Captain Marvel*, its first movie featuring a female hero as the sole lead (played by Oscar winner Brie Larson). "When we were just brainstorming ideas for what the story would be, I had this cover on our wall, this little-girl Captain Marvel, flying with her hands out and a huge smile on her face," director Anna Boden told *Entertainment Weekly* last year. "And we were like, 'We want to make little girls feel like that.'"

Those types of connections to the audience are as powerful as any dazzlingly bejeweled gauntlet a mad titan like Thanos might wield. A reminder of the strength of Marvel fans' passion came last October when Chris Evans tweeted that he had wrapped his work as Captain America on the upcoming *Avengers: Endgame*, signaling his expected departure from the MCU. "Playing this role over the last 8 years has been an honor," he wrote. "To everyone in front of the camera, behind the camera, and in the audience, thank you for the memories!" The message created an emotional tsunami across the internet, garnering more than 62,000 replies of gratitude and sadness and an astounding 1.4 million–plus "likes."

That kind of response is a reminder of the actual definition of the word "marvel," per Webster's dictionary, which perfectly sums up the world that Stan Lee and Co. began building all those years ago: "something that causes wonder or astonishment." □

CHAPTER 1

80

TRACING MARVEL'S PATH FROM HUMBLE COMIC-BOOK PUBLISHER TO DOMINATING FORCE IN ENTERTAINMENT

NTING

THE ORIGIN OF A SUPERHERO POWERHOUSE

OVER THE PAST 80 YEARS, MARVEL HAS BEEN AN AMBITIOUS COMIC-BOOK INNOVATOR, CREATING AN UNLIKELY EMPIRE THAT REVOLUTIONIZED THE POP-CULTURE LANDSCAPE

BY COURTNEY MIFSUD

IN THE LATE 1950S, THE OFFICES OF MARVEL COMics looked nothing like those of rival DC. The suited and glitzy DC brass had been owned by larger corporations for much of the company's life. Superman, Batman and Wonder Woman all made the Lexington Avenue–based publisher the industry leader. Marvel, then called Atlas Comics, with its single-room office down the hall from a porno mag, among other low-budget pulp titles, was trying and failing to imitate DC's success, until its visionary editor and his artists flipped the script.

"I was in several meetings with Mort [Weisinger, Superman editor in the 1950s and '60s] and a few people," Jim Shooter, Marvel's former editor in chief, who worked at DC in the 1960s, told Reed Tucker, author of *Slugfest: Inside the Epic, 50-Year Battle Between Marvel and DC*. "They were holding up the Marvel comics and ridiculing them. There was an issue of *X-Men* with a picture of [winged hero] Angel—a full-page shot—and the caption was all about the glory of flying. And their attitude was, 'What's the big deal? Superman flies all the time.' I'm like, 'Don't you get it? He flies all the time, and no one gives a damn.' One guy held up a *Spider-Man* and said, 'They've got two pages of Peter Parker talking to his aunt. The kids are going to be bored out of their minds.' Nope."

And bored they were not. When Marvel mixed its innovative editor-writer Stan Lee with the artistic greats Jack Kirby and Steve Ditko, comic books were changed forever. Their work survived decades of an alarmingly turbulent industry, and now the stories championed by these creators command screens of all sizes around the world.

THE FUTURE KING of Comics, Stan Lee was born Stanley Martin Lieber in New York City, the oldest child of a middle-class Jewish family. Jack, Stanley's father, was a dress cutter consistently struggling to find work during the Depression. "Seeing the demoralizing effect that his unemployment had on his spirit, making him feel that he just wasn't needed, gave me a feeling I've never been able to shake," Lee wrote in his first memoir, *Excelsior!*, published in 2002. "It's a feeling that the most important thing for a man is to have work to do, to be busy, to be needed."

The Lieber family relocated from Manhattan to the Bronx, where Stanley attended DeWitt Clinton High School and developed his writing skills. He wrote obituaries for a news service and worked on publicity materials for a hospital. After he finished high school, Lee's family couldn't afford to send him to college. But his cousin was married to magazine publisher Martin Goodman.

Marvel Comics wouldn't have existed without

"I've always thought of myself as being in show business," Lee once told TIME. *"It's just taken the world a long time to realize it."*

Lee quickly partnered with Jacob Kurtzberg, a writer-artist better known by his pen name, Jack Kirby. Five years Lee's senior, Kirby had already raked up a great deal of clout at Timely, particularly for co-creating Captain America, a Nazi-fighting supersoldier who became a major hit. The two couldn't have been more different. Lee was charismatic and handsome, known for leaping around the offices while playing an ocarina. Kirby, stocky and serious, was more often found crouched over his drawing board. And while Lee played nice with Goodman and the higher-ups, Kirby and editor in chief Joe Simon (who had created Captain America with Kirby) butted heads with Goodman and left the company in 1941. With a year on the job and not yet 19 years old, Lee was named editor in chief.

During the early 1940s, when America entered the war that Timely's characters had already been fighting, much of the staff joined the Army, including Lee. The comics industry worked hand in hand with the Office of War Information and the Writers' War Board. The civilian group had been founded to promote the sale of war bonds, but it functioned as a propaganda machine as well. Comics developed story arcs to foster American hatred for the enemy Axis powers. It is estimated that at least 44% of soldiers in training camps read comic books during the war and that the inexpensive and accessible medium inspired the troops with stories of unbreakable heroes. But although World War II and its aftermath marked the "golden age" of comics, the government's love affair with this medium wouldn't last.

The 1950s were a scary time for comic-book publishers. The fans had all but abandoned the genre's heroes, taking to other genres such as crime and horror stories and Westerns. The public was growing more and more worried about communist spies, driven by Senator Joseph McCarthy's 1953–54 Senate investigation. There was a moral panic about the comic industry's reported promotion of juvenile delinquency, which led to congressional hearings. Rather than accept government policing, the comics industry censored itself and created the Comics Code Authority to ensure that content was more wholesome. In the effort to strip out gore and moral ambiguity, witty writing and social issues were lost.

Goodman. A first-generation American born in Brooklyn, Goodman rose from his lowly roots in a poor immigrant family to become a successful publisher. By 1939 he was putting out dozens of magazines, on topics ranging from science to health to gunslinging, but he expanded into the world of comic books, a medium only just beginning to take off. Goodman gave Lee a job as an editorial gofer at Timely Comics in 1940, and soon the precocious teenager was writing scripts for upcoming titles.

*Fans paid tribute to Lee at his star on the Hollywood Walk of Fame in
Los Angeles following his death at age 95 last November.*

At Atlas Comics, the new name for Timely, Goodman had Lee following the successful trends of the time, grinding out generic Western and monster stories. It was not the work that Lee wanted to do, but it was the work that needed to be done to keep the lights on.

LEE'S BEST WORK was still ahead of him, and as the legend goes, it was all thanks to one fateful game of golf. According to Sean Howe's *Marvel Comics: The Untold Story*, Goodman took to the links with the head of DC Comics, Jack Liebowitz, who bragged about the successful collection of DC's leading heroes, the Justice League of America.

Not to be outdone, Goodman called on Lee to write his own superteam. Lee brought his concepts to Kirby, and they got to work on creating a squad that was nothing like what Goodman had asked for.

These heroes squabbled; they were flawed; they were human; they were the Fantastic Four.

"I've never been hit by lightning but I have to imagine the shock might be similar to what I experienced reading that early adventure of Reed Richards, Sue Storm, her kid brother Johnny, and Ben Grimm," wrote Gerry Conway, a comic writer who worked on *Spider-Man* and dozens of other titles over the past five decades. "If you weren't a comic book reader at that time you cannot imagine the impact those stories had. There's nothing comparable in the modern reader's experience of comics—nothing remotely as transformative. . . . Over a series of perhaps five issues, a single year, Stan and Jack Kirby transformed superhero comics in an act of creative alchemy similar to transmuting lead into gold, and just as unlikely."

Lee didn't want to create a band of heroes like DC's emotionally bland Justice League. Instead, he built a team that reflected real people. Lee conceived of the idea for the Fantastic Four and gave a typed-out pitch to Kirby to draw.

Kirby saw the origins of the Fantastic Four a little differently. He had returned to Timely in 1958 on a freelance basis and remarked how the company was not how he had left it. "I came in and they were moving out the furniture, they were taking desks out," Kirby told the *Comics Journal* in 1990. "Stan Lee is sitting on a chair crying. He didn't know what to do, he's sitting in a chair crying . . . I told him to stop crying. I says, 'Go in to Martin and tell him to stop moving the furniture out, and I'll see that the books make money.' " By Kirby's account, the quirky super-team was *his* idea.

Whoever came up with it, the comic was just what Goodman needed. *The Fantastic Four* No. 1 hit news-stands on Aug. 8, 1961, and the 25-page issue was a massive triumph. "Even before the sales totals were in, we knew we had a major success because of the amount of enthusiastic fan mail," Lee said in his most recent autobiography, *Amazing Fantastic Incredible: A Marvelous Memoir*. What Kirby and Lee accomplished over the ensuing months changed the comics game for decades to come. They would churn out hero after hero, like the marginalized X-Men, the misunderstood monster Hulk and the war profiteer Iron Man. "Almost everything I've ever written I could finish at one sitting," Lee once said, according to the *New York Times*. "I'm a fast writer. Maybe not the best, but the fastest."

In order to keep track of the weaving story lines, Lee decided to have most of these characters live in their fictional version of New York City, where they were constantly running into one another. "It's difficult to overstate the significance of Lee's invention of the idea of a comprehensive shared universe," wrote Vulture's Abraham Riesman in his 2016 essay "It's Stan Lee's Universe." "It was a genius way to move product: If you wanted the full story of what was going on with your favorite characters, you had to buy series that starred other characters."

The superhero who would ultimately define Lee's legacy was a shy high school student plagued with personal problems. Created with the artist Steve Ditko, the wisecracking Spider-Man, a.k.a. Peter Parker, swung onto the pages of *Amazing Fantasy* No. 15 in 1962. An immediate hit, the character has since transcended the comic-book medium, making the leap to television screens, movie theaters and video games over a span of decades.

It was during this era that Lee developed what he deemed "the Marvel method." Instead of handing artists fully realized scripts, he gave them summarized stories and let the artists figure out the plot details as they saw fit. Once the art came back to Lee, he'd work up the dialogue bubbles and sound effects. "Some artists, such as Jack Kirby, need no plot at all," Lee said in 1968. "I mean, I'll just say to Jack, 'Let's let the next villain be Dr. Doom.' Or I may not even say that. He may tell me. And then he goes home and does it. He's so good at plots, I'm sure he's a thousand times better than I."

Marvel's success exploded after Spider-Man swung onto the scene. Ditko developed the arrogant surgeon-turned-sorcerer Doctor Strange, and in September 1963 two game-changing supergroups arrived on the scene. The X-Men, a group of mutant teenagers rejected by society, subtly flicked at the civil rights struggles of the era. And the Avengers were a team-up of Marvel's superstars: Iron Man, Thor, the Hulk, Ant-Man and the Wasp (and, by the fourth issue, Captain America).

Thanks to a substantial increase in titles, Marvel passed DC in 1972 as the best-selling comic-book company in the world. And the behemoth still dominates. In 2018, Marvel held more than 38% of the market share of comic-book sales, while DC was runner-up, at 30%. "I was in an editorial meeting the first month that Marvel sales overtook DC's, and some of the old-timers were saying this was a temporary thing and we'd be back on top in a month or two," DC Comics writer Denny O'Neil told Tucker in *Slugfest*. "Well, that was 50 years ago, and DC has never been back on top, except for an isolated month here and there."

WITH AN EYE toward expanding Marvel into TV and film, Lee stepped down as editor in chief in 1972 and became publisher. He headed to Los Angeles in the late '70s as the company's brand ambassador to bring his comics to life. Many of the live-action TV and movies didn't work (except for *The Incredible Hulk*, which ran on CBS from 1977 to 1982). Without the confidence of the rest of the Marvel brass, Lee didn't have the authority to influence Hollywood producers, which made the move a struggle. "He was just a lone figure in the wilderness," Tom Spurgeon, a co-author of *Stan Lee and the Rise and Fall of the American Comic Book*, told Vulture. "He couldn't take a paper out of his jacket pocket and work out a deal there with anybody. He was a PR and concepts guy."

IN THE EARLY '90s, the comic-book industry faced rampant speculation. The supposed value for old and gimmicky limited-edition books created an inflated industry bubble, which burst after these trends failed to drive long-term sales. The market collapsed, and Marvel had to file Chapter 11 bankruptcy in 1996. Several tense legal battles later, upon having to pay back frustrated creators, the company was bolstered in 1997 thanks to a merger with Isaac Perlmutter's Toy Biz. One of Toy Biz's designers, Avi Arad, an Israel-born comic-book fan, was a champion of the potential value of Marvel characters. "Spider-Man alone is worth a billion dollars," he pleaded to bankers, as recounted in Dan Raviv's book *Comic Wars: Marvel's Battle for Survival*. "We have the X-Men. We have the Fantastic Four. They can all be movies."

By licensing some of its bigger properties, Marvel was able to emerge from bankruptcy. Perlmutter put some of the film rights on the auction block: Sony bought Spider-Man; Universal acquired the Hulk; 20th Century Fox gained the rights to the Fantastic Four, Daredevil and the X-Men.

Although many of these early movies were box-office successes, Marvel enjoyed only a relatively small percentage of the profits. Of the $3 billion that came from the first two Spider-Man movies in 2002 and '04, Marvel reportedly only received $62 million. The company had negotiated a modest flat fee from Fox for the X-Men franchise. "Mr. Perlmutter didn't expect to make much money off the movies, but he thought they'd make great advertisements for toys," Ben Fritz wrote in his book *The Big Picture: The Fight for the Future of Movies*. "The question wasn't who the kids would want to watch on the big screen, but which action figure would they want to play with. The answer was Iron Man."

Marvel promoted young producer Kevin Feige to president of production of its own studio in 2007, and the following year he brought Iron Man to life, with Robert Downey Jr. in the red-and-gold armor. "It starts with the comics and us getting to rip pages out, put them on the walls and start to be inspired," Feige said on the eve of the 2018 blockbuster *Avengers: Infinity War*. "It is always a guide point, a North Star for us as we lead these giant productions into reality." Though its titular star was considered by many to be a secondary character at best, *Iron Man*

grossed $585 million at the worldwide box office, and the Marvel Cinematic Universe was off and running.

Following the success of *Iron Man*, Disney bought Marvel for $4 billion in 2009. The sale gave Marvel the scale to pull off the ambitious multi-superhero, multi-film crossover plan that even Lee couldn't have imagined when he penned these original heroes in the '60s. *The Avengers*, uniting Iron Man, the Hulk, Thor, Captain America, Black Widow and Hawkeye in 2012, made billions and currently ranks as the sixth-highest-grossing movie of all time. The quirky 2014 space opera *Guardians of the Galaxy*, featuring obscure characters from the Marvel canon, was another risk that paid off. And last year's *Black Panther* smashed box-office records, earning $1.3 billion. The company simultaneously boasts a growing TV empire, with live-action and animated shows currently airing on ABC, Fox, FX, Freeform, Disney Channel, Netflix and Hulu.

Lee basked in the glory of Marvel's movie empire and delighted in making cameos in each of the films, popping up as everything from a bus driver to his own version of *Playboy* mogul Hugh Hefner. "Stan is right up there with Walt Disney as one of the great creators of not just one character but a whole galaxy of characters that have become part of our lives," *Game of Thrones* creator George R.R. Martin said in 2018. "Right now, I think he's probably bigger than Disney."

STAN LEE DIED on Nov. 12, 2018, at age 95. "How many millions of us are indebted to this guy, none more so than me," Tom Holland, the latest actor to play Spider-Man, wrote on Instagram. "The father of Marvel has made so many people so incredibly happy. What a life and what a thing to have achieved. Rest in peace Stan."

Marvel, though, has not slowed. The year 2019 features the release of *Captain Marvel*, with the universe's most powerful hero (played by Academy Award winner Brie Larson), and the fourth *Avengers* film. And the Marvel universe will continue to live on beyond its creators, thanks to the unlikely foundation set decades ago in that unspectacular Manhattan office. "I want to do more movies, I want to do more television, more DVDs, more multi-sodes, I want to do more lecturing, I want to do more of everything I'm doing," Lee said in the 2010 documentary *With Great Power: The Stan Lee Story*. "The only problem is time. I just wish there were more time." □

Giving Credit to Marvel's Unsung Artistic Heroes

BY COURTNEY MIFSUD

Although Stan Lee is lauded as the father of Marvel Comics, the impact of two artists, Jack Kirby and Steve Ditko, who worked with Lee in the 1960s to develop some of the publisher's most iconic characters, cannot be understated.

Born Jacob Kurtzberg in 1917, Kirby (right) grew up in crowded tenements in New York City. He got his start in the comics industry in the 1930s, eventually teaming up with fellow artist Joe Simon, who would be his partner for 15 years. Together they created Captain America, who made his Timely Comics debut in 1940 by delivering a punch to Adolf Hitler on the cover. After serving in World War II, Kirby worked for numerous publishers before returning to work for Martin Goodman at Atlas Comics (as Timely was by then called). He teamed up with Lee to develop and co-plot the Fantastic Four before crafting other characters such as Silver Surfer and Black Panther with his signature dynamic style. "Jack Kirby is comics," Mitch Gerads, who illustrated a DC Comics reboot of Kirby's Mister Miracle, told *Entertainment Weekly* in 2017. "Everything we love about comics, from the line art to the writing, you can't have it without Jack Kirby."

Like Lee's work with Kirby, the story of a cornerstone Marvel hero, Spider-Man, can't be told without Steve Ditko. Born in 1927 in Johnstown, Pa., Ditko graduated from high school in 1945 and then joined the Army in postwar Germany, where he drew cartoons for a service newspaper. After returning home, Ditko illustrated various print projects, mainly horror-, crime- and science-fiction-driven. Comic-book writer Alan Moore said in a 2007 British documentary that in Ditko's work there was "a tormented

elegance to the way the characters stood, the way that they bent their hands," adding, "They always looked as if they were on the edge of some kind of revelation or breakdown."

Ditko's proficiency, along with his speed, impressed Stan Lee, who hired him at Atlas. The most notable of Ditko's co-creations was Spider-Man, the costumed alias of nerdy teenager Peter Parker, who first appeared in 1962. "All of this was balanced, brilliantly and precariously, with breezy acrobatic action sequences," wrote Sean Howe in *Marvel Comics: The Untold Story*. "Ditko's rendering of athleticism was quite different from Kirby's, more about gymnastic dodging than knockout punches, but it was just as exciting." Ditko was also the driving force behind Doctor Strange, a mystical superhero who debuted in 1963.

Controversy surrounding the origins of these iconic characters dogs the legacies of Lee, Kirby and Ditko. Lee has often been hailed as the sole creator of Spider-Man and the Fantastic Four, under the widely circulated—and

incorrect—assumption that Kirby and Ditko merely drew up his ideas. As Lee's star rose, both artists eventually left Marvel disgruntled over compensation and credit. But according to Lee, he gave artists their fair due. "I always tried to show them in the most favorable light, even in the credits," Lee told *Playboy* in 2014. "There was never a time when it just said 'by Stan Lee.' It was always 'by Stan Lee and Steve Ditko' or 'by Stan Lee and Jack Kirby.' I made sure their names were always as big as mine. . . . I'm sorry anybody feels there's any acrimony. I loved them both."

Kirby, who returned to Marvel after a stint at DC Comics, died in 1994 at the age of 76. Ditko did occasional work for DC and Marvel and produced independent comics out of the public eye up until his death in 2018 at the age of 90. Despite Lee getting the most time in the spotlight, Kirby and Ditko have long been lauded within the comics community for their integral contributions to building the Marvel universe, shaping stories that have captivated the world.

SPIDEY SAVES THE DAY

DESPITE OBJECTIONS FROM HIS BOSS, STAN LEE CRAFTED A PLAN TO GIVE LIFE TO AN UNLIKELY SUPERHERO. LITTLE DID HE KNOW THAT A LEGEND WAS ABOUT TO BE BORN

BY BOB BATCHELOR

THE 1962 DEBUT OF SPIDER-MAN IN *AMAZING FANtasy* No. 15 happened because Stan Lee took a calculated risk. He trusted his instincts, honed over decades of working in the chaotic comic-book industry, which often seemed to run on trial and error more than logic. On the long path from idea to the newsstands, sales determined what each publisher offered. Fickle comic-book fans frequently switched interests, leaving editors like Lee scratching their heads and trying to predict the next fad.

Rolling the dice on a new character also meant potentially wasting precious hours writing, penciling and inking a title that might not sell when that same time could be used on more profitable books. In an industry driven by talent and always against the clock, there were never enough good artists and writers to spare time for a series that did not sell. The business side of the industry constantly clashed with the creative aspects, forcing fast scripting and artwork to go hand in hand. The creative teams always raced against stringent monthly deadlines.

In more than two decades toiling away as a comic-book writer and editor, Lee watched genres spring to life, and then almost as quickly, readers would turn their attention to something else. War stories might give way to romance titles, which would then ride a wave until monster comics became popular, and then be superseded by aliens. In an era when a small group of publishers controlled the entire industry, they kept close watch over each other's products in hopes of mimicking sales of hot titles.

Lee called Marvel publisher Martin Goodman "one of the great imitators of all time." Goodman dictated what Lee wrote and published after ferret-

One of the most iconic comic books of all time, *Amazing Fantasy* No. 15 introduced the world to Peter Parker and his alter ego, Spider-Man. The story featured the memorable line "with great power there must also come great responsibility," which has become a signature catchphrase associated with the character. A near-mint-condition copy of the issue sold at auction for $1.1 million in 2011.

ing out tips and leads from golf matches and long lunches with other publishers. If he heard that Westerns were selling for a competitor, Goodman would visit Lee, bellowing, "Stan, come up with some Westerns." Every new fad meant immediately switching to those kinds of titles. The versatility necessary in this environment had been Lee's primary strength, based on swift writing and plotting many different titles almost simultaneously and hiring teams of fast writers and artists to fill in the gaps. Lee had been working under these conditions for so long that he had mastered the techniques for easily creating multiple story lines and plots, using gimmicks and wordplay to remember names and titles, like recycling the gunslinger Rawhide Kid in 1960 and making him into an outlaw or using alliteration, as in Millie the Model.

When certain comic genres sold well, Goodman gave Lee breathing room, but when sales dipped, he put pressure on his editor. A conservative executive, Goodman rarely wanted change, which irked Lee. The writer bristled at his boss's belittling beliefs, explaining, "He felt comics were really only read by very, very young children or stupid adults," which meant "he didn't want me to use words of more than two syllables if I could help it. . . . Don't play up characterization, don't have too much dialogue, just have a lot of action." Given the precarious state of individual publishing companies, which frequently went belly-up, and his long history with Goodman, Lee admitted, "It was a job; I had to do what he told me."

Despite being distant relatives and longtime co-workers, the publisher and editor maintained a cool relationship. From Lee's perspective, "Martin was good at what he did and made a lot of money, but he wasn't ambitious. He wanted things to stay the way they were."

Riding the wave of critical success and extraordinary sales of *The Fantastic Four*, Goodman gave Lee a simple directive in line with his general management style: "Come up with some other superheroes." For the publisher, the order made sense: superheroes seemed to be the next big genre to catch on, so that would be Timely's new direction. Yet *The Fantastic Four* subtly shifted the relationship between editor and publisher. With sales doubling because of the new superhero team, Goodman looked away a bit, which enabled Lee to wield greater influence and authority. From the publisher's perspective, the popularity of superhero books meant simply jumping on the bandwagon until it died out. Lee, though, used

some of the profit to pay freelance writers and editors more money, which then off-loaded some of the pressure he felt in writing, plotting, editing, overseeing artwork and approving the company's limited number of monthly titles. In launching Spider-Man, however, Lee did more than divert the talents and energy of his staff. He actually defied Goodman.

For months, Lee had grappled with the idea of a new kind of superhero in the same vein as the Fantastic Four, with realistic challenges that someone with superpowers would experience living in the modern world. The new character, however, would be "a teenager, with all the problems, hang-ups and angst of any teenager." Lee came up with the colorful "Spider-Man" name and envisioned a "hard-luck kid" both blessed and cursed by acquiring superhuman strength and the ability to cling to walls, sides of buildings and even ceilings, just like a real-life spider. He knew Spider-Man would be an important character for the company and its efforts in the superhero genre.

Lee recalled going to see Goodman: "I did what I always did in those days, I took the idea to my boss, my friend, my publisher, my cohort," even embellishing the story of Spider-Man's origin by claiming that he had gotten the idea from "watching a fly on the wall while I had been typing." He laid the character out in full: teen, orphan, angst, poor, intelligent and other traits the young man would possess. Lee thought Spider-Man was a no-brainer, but to his surprise, Goodman hated it and forbade him from offering it as a stand-alone comic book.

The longtime publisher had three major complaints: "people hate spiders, so you can't call a hero 'Spider-Man'"; no teenager could be a hero "but only be a sidekick"; and a hero had to be heroic, not a pimply kid who isn't popular or strong. To Goodman, a hero who isn't a hero or even particularly likable sounded like a "comedy character." Irritated, he asked Lee, "Didn't [he] realize that people hate spiders?" Given the litany of criticisms, Lee recalled, "Martin just wouldn't let me do the book."

Goodman thought featuring a teenager would also make his company a laughingstock among comic-book publishers, a concern that the executive worried about incessantly. No matter what the company's success, Goodman felt the ups and downs of the industry too keenly, so he pushed back on ideas that he thought would fizzle and kept looking to pick up on the successes of other publishers. Goodman hated everything about Spider-Man. He usually took a hands-on approach only during downturns, but when Lee brought him the new character, the writer opened himself up to Goodman's insecurities and fears regarding status in the marketplace and among competitors.

Realizing that he could not completely circumvent his boss, Lee made the executive decision to at least give Spider-Man a try in as low-risk a manner as possible. The best case for the experiment would be to place the character on the cover of a series that had bombed up to that point—*Amazing Fantasy*. The comic-buying public simply had little interest in the *AF* run, which usually featured thriller/fantasy stories by Lee and surreal art by Steve Ditko, Marvel's go-to artist for styling the macabre, surreal or Dali-esque. At one point, Lee even put the word "Adult" directly into the title, hoping that "*Amazing Adult Fantasy*" would get readers interested. Facing Goodman's disdain and the woeful *AF* sales figures, it seemed as if there were already two strikes against the teen wonder.

Despite these odds and his boss's directive, Lee remembered that he couldn't let the nerdy superhero go, saying, "I couldn't get Spider-Man out of my mind." He worked up a Spider-Man plot and handed it over to legendary artist Jack Kirby. Lee figured that no one would care about (or maybe even notice) a new character in the last issue of a series that would soon be discontinued.

In this fast-paced environment, where Lee served essentially as Marvel's managing editor, writer, copy editor and overall creative director, he turned to artists he trusted because they needed little direction and worked quickly. Often, Lee would dictate a story line or just provide a fragment of the story and then

Nearly six decades after his debut, Lee's iconic hero still stars in multiple Marvel comics each month.

the artist would take that plot and begin to draw the issue. Later, the writer would add the dialogue and extra information, allowing time to edit or add in what the artist might have overlooked.

With Spider-Man, however, Kirby missed the mark. His early sketches turned the teen bookworm into a mini-Superman with all-American good looks, like a budding astronaut or football star. With little time to pause and think about what was essentially a throwaway character, Kirby turned to other projects and Lee put Ditko on the title. He did the art for *Amazing Fantasy* anyway, and his style was more suited for drawing an offbeat hero.

Ditko nailed Spider-Man, but not the cover art, forcing Lee to commission Kirby for the task, with Ditko inking. Despite needing Kirby's last-minute effort on the cover, Lee could not have been happier with Ditko's version of the teen. He explained: "Steve did a totally brilliant job of bringing my new little arachnid hero to life." They finished the two-part story and ran it as the lead in *AF* No. 15. Revealing both the busy, all-hands state of the company and their low expectations, Lee recalled, "Then, we more or less forgot about him." As happy as Lee and Ditko were with the collaboration and outcome, there is no way they could have imagined that they were about to spin the comic-book world onto a different axis.

THE HECTIC PACE of the comic-book business did not allow anyone to slow down, let alone stop to contemplate how the public might react to a particular title. Lee and his small crew of artists were already off onto new titles, working against the relentless deadlines.

Although the sales figures would be unavailable for several months, Lee realized that Spider-Man had found an audience when letters from readers poured into the office, just as they had a year earlier when the Fantastic Four debuted. Lee recalled getting about a hundred fan letters a day and sometimes more, which he dutifully read and answered.

The fateful day that sales figures finally arrived, Goodman stormed into Lee's office, as always awash in art boards, drawings, mock-ups, yellow legal pads and memos littering his desk.

Goodman beamed, "Stan, remember that Spider-Man idea of yours that I liked so much? Why don't we turn it into a series?"

If that wasn't enough to knock Lee off kilter, then came the real kicker: Spider-Man was not just a hit; the issue was in fact the fastest-selling comic book of the year, and indeed the decade. *Amazing Fantasy*, perpetually at the bottom of the sales charts, skyrocketed to No. 1 with issue No. 15, due to Lee's efforts to bring the character to life. Although it had been months since Lee and Ditko had created Spider-Man, the overwhelming popularity meant that the creative team would need to begin work immediately to turn the character into a series.

Despite Goodman's initial negativity and the indifference Kirby had about drawing Spider-Man, the success of *Amazing Fantasy* No. 15 elevated Lee and Ditko, since the new character would be the keystone of Marvel's superhero-based lineup. More important, the combination of the Fantastic Four and Spider-Man transformed Marvel from a company run by imitating trends of other publishers to a hip and relevant hot commodity.

Because of the long lag in obtaining sales figures and the length of the printing and distribution system, it wasn't until six months later that the new Spidey comic book debuted. To make way for the new title, Lee had to drop one, since the company's distribution agreement with Independent News allowed Marvel to carry only eight titles. Thus, a little less than a year after its debut, *The Incredible Hulk* ceased publication based on limited sales. In March 1963, *The Amazing Spider-Man* No. 1 burst onto newsstands. ☐

All Hail Stan Lee, the King of Cameos

BY RICH SANDS

Nobody loved the spotlight more than Stan Lee, who reveled in his opportunities to make cameo appearances in Marvel films (including 2019 posthumous appearances in *Captain Marvel* and *Avengers: Endgame*). Thanks to his celebrity status, he was also an in-demand guest star on a variety of non-Marvel movies and TV shows.

△ In a 2017 episode of the ABC sitcom *Fresh Off the Boat*, Lee played himself, reviewing comic-book submissions.

"I think I know that guy," Lee says, pointing to the late-arriving Peter Parker (Andrew Garfield) at his high school graduation in 2014's *The Amazing Spider-Man 2.* "He would show up to the movie sets game for anything," Marvel Studios president Kevin Feige told *Entertainment Weekly* last year. "But one thing he would always do is try to add more lines. He always would joke—but not really joke—about wanting more lines."

In the first *Fantastic Four* film (2005), he played mailman Willie Lumpkin—a character Lee co-created—delivering a pile of past-due bills to Reed Richards/Mister Fantastic (Ioan Gruffudd) and Sue Storm/Invisible Woman (Jessica Alba) at the Baxter Building. Among the other roles he played in Marvel movies were a general, a librarian, a bartender, a school-bus driver, several innocent bystanders and, of course, himself.

Lee made several appearances on the animated Fox hit *The Simpsons,* including a 2014 episode in which an imaginary version of himself encourages the sad and lonely Comic Book Guy to ask a woman out. When CBG complains that he's interfering, Lee responds, "Hey, I'm 90 years old, I can do what I want."

The *Big Bang Theory* gang were all huge fans of the comic-book legend, and they got to meet him in a 2010 episode of the CBS comedy that was appropriately titled "The Excelsior Acquisition" as an homage to one of Lee's trademark exclamations.

A COLLECTION OF ICONIC ISSUES

WHEN IT COMES TO THESE CELEBRATED STORIES, YOU *CAN* JUDGE A COMIC BY ITS COVER

The X-Men No. 1 (1963)
Stan Lee and Jack Kirby introduced the team of superpowered mutants, led by Professor Xavier. The squad included Cyclops, Beast, Iceman, Angel and Marvel Girl.

The Incredible Hulk No. 181 (1974)
Wolverine, arguably the most popular member of the X-Men, made his debut here, flashing his trademark adamantium claws while battling the Hulk in the Canadian wilderness.

Captain America Comics No. 1 (1940)

Before there was Marvel Comics, the publisher was known as Timely. One of the company's first superheroes was the patriotic Captain America, who splashed onto the scene during World War II to battle Nazis, thanks to Joe Simon and Jack Kirby. The character returned in 1964 in the pages of *Avengers* No. 4, after having been frozen since the war.

The Uncanny X-Men No. 135 (1980)
"The Dark Phoenix Saga," by Chris Claremont and John Byrne, kicked into high gear in this issue as telepath Jean Grey became corrupted by a cosmic entity and went on an intergalactic rampage. The upcoming film *Dark Phoenix* (starring *Game of Thrones*'s Sophie Turner) is based on this arc.

The Amazing Spider-Man No. 33 (1966)
Widely considered one of Spidey's greatest stories, "If This Be My Destiny" concluded in this issue, with the hero struggling to break free under fallen steel during a gut-wrenching five-page sequence by artist Steve Ditko. An homage to the momentous scene was featured in the 2017 film *Spider-Man: Homecoming*.

Captain Marvel No. 1 (2012)
Writer Kelly Sue DeConnick gave Carol Danvers—the Avenger formerly known as Ms. Marvel—an empowering makeover in this reboot, solidifying her status as one of the Marvel universe's most powerful heroes, as she reluctantly took on a new moniker.

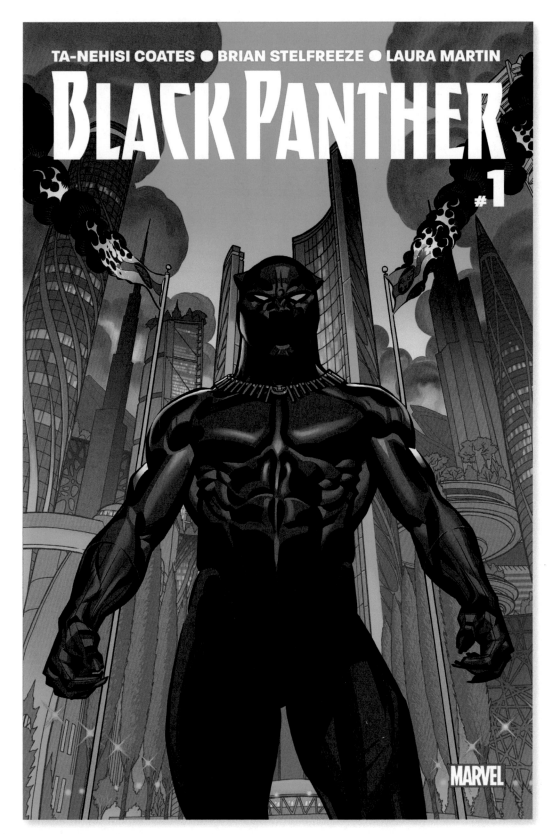

Black Panther No. 1 (2016)
The King of Wakanda got a high-profile launch when National Book Award winner Ta-Nehisi Coates began writing a new Black Panther series, bringing the reader inside the political intrigue of a divided and war-torn country. "It is not enough to be the sword," T'Challa was told, "you must be the intelligence behind it."

CHAPTER 2

MARVEL

**BEHIND THE SCENES
OF THE BIRTH
AND GROWTH OF
AN AMBITIOUS
ONSCREEN
UNIVERSE**

HOLL

GOES

YWOOD

THE MAN BEHIND THE MOVIES

MARVEL STUDIOS PRESIDENT KEVIN FEIGE WORKED HIS WAY TO THE TOP OF HOLLYWOOD BY RESPECTING THE COMIC-BOOK LORE AND TAKING CHANCES ON UNHERALDED HEROES

BY ANTHONY BREZNICAN

THE MARVEL CINEMATIC UNIVERSE BEGAN, AS ALL universes do, with a massive void, intense pressure and suddenly—a spark.

There was a period of time, long before every studio in Hollywood wanted to follow Marvel Studios' lead and create its own ever-expanding interlocked series of movies, when that idea was preposterous, foolhardy and fraught with danger. One weak link could unravel everything, leading to big-budget bombs, bankruptcy and indefinitely damaged characters.

Turning one superhero film into a hit was hard enough, but keeping it going? Even Batman couldn't manage that feat. Banking on one obscure character opening the door for another, then another, and finally uniting them all in one epic climax? That was crazy. A no-go. No sane studio head would under-

write such a reckless experiment.

So Marvel went it alone.

In 2004, the film arm of the comic-book company launched its own studio. No longer interested in licensing their characters to others, the Marvel execs planned to use the heroes they still owned to build a five-movie bridge from *Iron Man* to *The Incredible Hulk* to *Iron Man 2* to *Thor*, then *Captain America* and finally *The Avengers*. Now, a decade later, that experiment is more successful than any of its engineers could have imagined, sprinting toward 2019's movies No. 21 (*Captain Marvel*) and No. 22 (*Avengers: Endgame*) with $17.5 billion in lifetime global box office and no end in sight.

How it got to this point is an epic story on its own. And it all hinged on the actions of a quiet kid from New Jersey.

"The notion of an ending, the notion of a finale, became very intriguing to us, in large part because you don't see it that often in this particular genre."
—Kevin Feige, on
Avengers: Endgame

THE VOID

TODAY, FANS KNOW KEVIN FEIGE AS THE baseball-cap-wearing president of Marvel Studios, a 21st-century variation on Stan Lee who took that iconic comic scribe's collaborations and put them onscreen as the chief architect of the Marvel Cinematic Universe.

In 1997, he was a 24-year-old production assistant on the Warner Bros. lot who had graduated just two years earlier from the University of Southern California's film school. Raised in Westfield, N.J., Feige went to school in Los Angeles because he was a lifelong movie lover, and he entered the business, ironically, just as the superhero genre was starting to collapse.

His first job was with Lauren Shuler Donner, the producer of *Ladyhawke, Pretty in Pink* and *St. Elmo's Fire* and the wife and producing partner of *Superman* director Richard Donner. Feige's first credit was as Shuler Donner's assistant on the 1997 Tommy Lee Jones disaster film *Volcano*, about an eruption of lava in the middle of Los Angeles. That movie came out about two months before a metaphorical disaster struck Hollywood—*Batman & Robin*, which was such box-office poison that it killed off the entire franchise and soured moviegoers on superheroes.

"Lauren and Dick's company was based at Warner Bros., so there was a lot of Batman," Feige recalls. "I remember seeing the Gotham City back lot, Batmobile chases and things like that. It was always very exciting that that was happening. That movie didn't work, obviously, and underperformed, and it was kind of like, 'Well, that's the end of that,' in terms of movies based on comic books." This was alarming for the Donners. One of their major movies in development was a big-screen version of Marvel's X-Men comics.

Feige admits he was not a lifelong fan steeped in the nuances of decades of comic-book lore. But he was a fast learner. "I knew Superman. I knew Batman. I knew Spider-Man from cartoons. I knew Hulk from the old TV series," Feige says. "All of my deep-diving of comics in my adulthood was based on, How could this fit into a feature? How could I fit this frame, this line, this theme, this story into the structure of a feature film?"

Eager to prove himself, Feige dug deep into classic X-Men comic-book runs, hoping to add some value to the film that was entering a marketplace where superhero stories were considered damaged goods. "While I loved being involved in movies in any capacity with *Volcano* and *You've Got Mail*, I was looking for something that I could grow with and be more additive to and more helpful with," Feige recalls. "I started writing notes on the early drafts of *X-Men* that came in, and because Lauren is an amazing mentor and is so gracious, she would read the notes. Eventually, she started saying, 'Hey, come into the office and sit with me.' I would be sitting with Tom DeSanto, who's the producer of *X-Men*, and Bryan Singer, who was the newly hired director, and I just started to become a part of that creative team."

Many of his early contributions to the story were as a historian. "I would just start digging even further into the comics and go, 'Well, look at this. There's a lot of great stuff here,' " Feige says. "I would raise a red flag, like with Wolverine's hair on the first couple of days of production. It didn't feel like Wolverine's hair [from the comics]." To his surprise, the filmmakers changed it.

When *X-Men* hit theaters in 2000, it carried a new credit for Feige: associate producer. And Avi Arad, then president of Marvel Studios, hired him to continue with the company.

X-Men was a gargantuan hit, and comic-book movies were suddenly back in vogue. "[Arad] said, 'OK, we're making a lot of movies of these,' " Feige recalls. Arad was based in New York, so his young new hire got to be Marvel's main rep in Los Angeles.

When the first draft of a *Spider-Man* script came in, he was dispatched to Sony Pictures to discuss it with producer Laura Ziskin and director Sam Raimi. "Who the hell am I? Nobody," Feige recalls. "So I sat in there and didn't open my mouth. I just listened." As more movies were added to the Marvel slate, he learned a lot more than just how to make one film. "In hindsight," he says, "there couldn't have been a better way to have started a new studio."

THE PRESSURE

AT THIS POINT, MARVEL WAS STILL JUST TRYING to get other studios to make movies based on its heroes and villains. Looking back, Feige sees a frustrating contradiction. "It doesn't make any sense," he says. "You've licensed your characters out to every other studio in town, and then you spend the next 10, 15, 20 years trying to get them back when you become your own studio."

During those early years, he helped Fox make *X2: X-Men United, Daredevil, Elektra* and 2005's *Fantas-*

tic Four. He was an executive producer of Universal's *Hulk* (directed by Ang Lee) in 2003 and Sony's *Spider-Man 2* in 2004. "I got to spend my first six years or so at Marvel working with almost every single studio in town," he says. Feige worked on more than a dozen films, and he says each was a critical learning experience—even if the finished film was sometimes a wreck. "I was seeing when things were done well, things that I'd want to emulate, and seeing fear-based decisions or Monday-morning quarterbacking that didn't work so well," he notes.

The job became more difficult as Marvel tried to license some of its less-iconic heroes. Iron Man was considered a B-lister; how about Thor? Captain America? Ant-Man? Who were they? Studios were less interested in gambling on those longtime characters, let alone something as absurd as a talking raccoon and a warrior tree in *Guardians of the Galaxy*.

It was hard enough to stop studios from messing up the things they liked. "There was a lot of time spent in those early years trying to convince the people who were in charge of the studios why there should be horns on Daredevil's cowl, things like that," Feige says. "Sometimes they would agree with us, and sometimes they wouldn't. It was always frustrating to me to spend time trying to convince people, as opposed to just being able to do it."

Marvel's powers that be agreed. Then they came up with what would become known as the Big Idea— they would stop asking, and start making the movies themselves.

THE SPARK

THE ORIGINAL PLAN WAS JUST TO MAKE STAND-alone films. That's the point at which two other critical names joined the list: director Jon Favreau and star Robert Downey Jr., whose charm as Tony Stark rivals the power of any Infinity Stone. "All we were doing [was] trying to make our first two movies, *Iron Man* and *The Incredible Hulk*," Feige says. "That was 99% the focus."

In the midst of production on *Iron Man*, Feige—then elevated to president of Marvel Studios—got a phone call. It was Samuel L. Jackson's agent. "In the comic books, in the Ultimate line, they had started drawing Nick Fury as identical, looking exactly like Sam Jackson," Feige says. "Sam is a big fan, and he agreed to come and shoot that cameo."

In that cameo, the first of the MCU's post-credit scenes, Tony Stark returns home to find a stranger with an eye patch in his home. "You've become part of a bigger universe," Fury tells him. "You just don't know it yet."

That's the phrase that ignited imaginations and led, over the next decade, to the introduction of not just the core Avengers but also Black Panther, Doctor Strange and Captain Marvel. That initial idea of a connected series of movies was so audacious that in the years before Disney acquired Marvel, other studios didn't believe it. "I think it seemed so crazy that they literally didn't register," Feige says. "What's the worst that would happen? It would bomb, and we wouldn't be a studio. Well, we weren't a studio before that."

The "bigger universe" scene was tacked on at the end of *Iron Man* so it wouldn't be distracting. "But we knew that, yes, we didn't have X-Men or Fantastic Four or Spider-Man, who were the most popular characters, but we had everything else, which not only meant Avengers but meant interlocking an actual universe for the first time," Feige says. "That's what the comics were all about. You flip a page in one person's book, and another character is going to appear."

Eleven years in, Feige has managed an impressive act of continuity with the series. "Things only happen arbitrarily in Kevin Feige's Marvel universe by mistake, and I think he's maybe made two mistakes," Downey told *Entertainment Weekly* on the set of 2015's *Avengers: Age of Ultron*. He's talking about little references, like an Infinity Gauntlet turning up in Odin's trophy room in 2011's *Thor* (which had to be dismissed as a fake in 2017's *Thor: Ragnarok* in order for the *Infinity War* story to line up). "They were more like Easter eggs early on," Downey said. "Things that he didn't have as much final say over but would nowadays." Even the title *Endgame* was referenced not just by Doctor Strange's dialogue in *Infinity War* but also by a warning from Tony Stark in *Age of Ultron*, about the greatest threat to Earth coming from the unknown reaches of space.

Now that the Marvel Cinematic Universe has come so far, what threats await its heroes in the years to come? Feige has a plan, but he's not revealing it just yet. All he's issuing is a warning. "*Endgame* is the title for a reason," he says. "Here's another thing that these kind of films with iconic characters, 'franchise characters,' don't usually get—a finale."

At the edge of every universe, however, another must begin. □

READY FOR HER CLOSE-UP

POTENTIALLY THE MOST POWERFUL HERO IN THE UNIVERSE, CAPTAIN MARVEL IS SET TO SOAR ABOVE THE EXPECTATIONS OF A MALE-DOMINATED GENRE

BY ELIANA DOCKTERMAN

INFINITY WAR SERIOUSLY THINNED THE NUMBER of superheroes who can take on Thanos in the fourth *Avengers* film. If the superpowered team plans to defeat the Infinity Gauntlet–wielding alien, it will need backup.

Enter Captain Marvel, Marvel's first female superhero to get a solo film. Her eponymous epic, set in the 1990s, outlines the character's origin story: Carol Danvers is a fighter pilot with alien powers. She can fly, shoot beams from her hands and pack a major punch. In short, she's the most powerful superhero in the Marvel Cinematic Universe.

There are seven weeks between the debuts of *Captain Marvel* and *Avengers: Endgame*, and her presence in *Endgame* was presaged in 2018's *Infinity War*: Nick Fury sends her an SOS signal on a pager when he realizes that Thanos is destroying half of all life in the universe.

Fans have been begging Marvel for a female superhero film ever since they spotted Scarlett Johansson as Black Widow in *Iron Man 2* in 2010. But back then, many studio executives still considered female comic-book movies a risky bet. Flops like *Catwoman* and *Elektra* lent to the notion that the teen boys who made up much of the superhero-movie audience simply wouldn't be interested in watching a woman save the world. In leaked Sony emails from 2014, a Marvel executive called female superhero movies a "disaster." So for years, onscreen crime fighters remained male, white and straight. Occasionally, sidekick or villain characters broke that mold, but never did they get their own films.

Of course, *Catwoman* and *Elektra* were simply

Brie Larson spent time with Air Force pilots, including going up in an F-16 fighter jet, to prepare for the role of Carol Danvers.

terrible movies. As soon as studios began to green-light good genre movies with female leads, audiences upended the old misogynist view. *The Hunger Games* proved that female heroes could draw massive audiences. *Star Wars: The Force Awakens*, starring Daisy Ridley as the first prominent female Jedi, broke box-office records. *Mad Max: Fury Road* showed that a provocative female character could upstage her male counterpart, even if he's the one with the decades-old fan following.

In 2016, Marvel announced that Brie Larson, fresh off a Best Actress Oscar win for *Room*, would portray Captain Marvel in a 2018 film. But the movie was delayed until 2019, and in any case, Warner Bros. beat Marvel Studios to the punch: DC's Wonder Woman made her big-screen debut in 2017.

The critical and commercial success of that film has taken some pressure off *Captain Marvel*. *Wonder Woman* set several records, including highest-grossing live-action film directed by a woman. In theory, the success of *Wonder Woman* put the tiresome debate about whether a female superhero movie could succeed to rest. But as the trailblazer, *Wonder Woman* had to tread carefully: her costume could neither be too sexy nor too masculine, her philosophy neither conservative nor pugnacious. Wonder Woman, originally conceived during World War II, is a distinctly feminine hero: She wears heels and a skirt. She falls for Steve Trevor. She preaches love and peace. Her power is awe-inspiring, not frightening. As a result, she had to contend with criticism from feminists that she was too sexy and too passive, while dodging comments from misogynists who didn't want to see any woman in power onscreen.

Captain Marvel is a completely different character from Wonder Woman, and even before her debut she has faced an entirely new set of criticisms. She's a control freak with a big ego and a bit of a temper. She's occasionally reckless and delightfully unconcerned with making anyone around her feel comfortable. And as internet trolls have noted in the comments section of the *Captain Marvel* trailers, she doesn't smile.

Telling a woman to smile more is a favorite tactic of misogynists, and a cohort of Twitter provocateurs quickly latched onto Larson's stoic visage when the teaser premiered. The actress fired back a response on Instagram: "Breaking news: You can be you. That means you can smile or not. You can be strong in the

"When she's introduced, she will be by far the strongest character we've ever had," declared Marvel Studios president Kevin Feige.

ways you want to be. You can own who you are. If anyone tells you different don't trust them."

Even as female moviegoers bask in *Wonder Woman*'s success, the sexist response of a small but loud minority acts as a sobering reminder that society still places certain strictures on female strength. Captain Marvel's costume is refreshingly masculine in a movie landscape where so-called female badasses are often clad in leather or short skirts. She intimidates men and revels in that power. In short, audiences have spent decades watching men's conceptions of female power: women who are strong but not too strong, intimidating but still sexually appealing, hardened but vulnerable under the surface.

Captain Marvel violates a lot of those notions, and it's about time someone like her saved us all.

THE CAPTAIN MARVEL moniker originally belonged to a man. Carol Danvers was just a side character in his story, an officer in the U.S. Air Force. In the 1970s, Carol got powers and a promotion. She took on the name of Ms. Marvel, a nod to the feminist publication *Ms.* magazine. She worked as a fighter pilot, a NASA scientist and the editor of a women's magazine who wore scarves and oversize glasses in unabashed tribute to *Ms.* co-founder Gloria Steinem.

But in the decades that followed, Carol lost much of her swagger. Her superhero outfit, a bathing suit with thigh-high boots, was clearly designed to be ogled, not admired. Finally, in 2012, writer Kelly Sue DeConnick gave Carol a more modern redesign and the Captain Marvel name. (The previous standard-bearer had been dead for years in the comics.) Artist Jamie McKelvie reimagined the costume and gave her a more practical look inspired by her military past, complete with a short Mohawk-esque hairstyle.

Carol is a good role model, though not a perfect one. Her father believed that sending women to college was a waste of money, so she joined the Air Force and has been driven by a desire to prove herself better, smarter and faster than the boys. As DeConnick has succinctly said, when Captain America falls down, he gets up because it's the right thing to do; Captain Marvel gets back up because she's thinking "f--- you" to the person who hit her.

Few writers imbue female action heroes with such complexity. The women warriors onscreen are often "badass" in the same sort of cliché way: they drink hard, act like one of the boys and zip around on a motorcycle in spandex—but their heart eventually melts when they fall for the hero. Many action-movie screenwriters still assiduously avoid any trait that might render a woman "unlikable" and populate their movies with bland women. "The test that I always give young writers is, if you can take out your female character and replace her with a sexy lamp and your plot still functions, you're doing it wrong," DeConnick told TIME in 2014.

Captain Marvel represents a break from those walking clichés. That's crucial because girls and boys need more female role models onscreen. Right now, the dearth of female superheroes forces girls to learn to identify with male heroes. Boys are never forced to do the same. The result: men who run studios don't feel they can relate to women, and thus they don't make movies about women. It's a self-perpetuating cycle.

"Everyone wants to identify up, to aspire up," DeConnick said in the same interview. "So if you are female and therefore lower status in terms of your cultural power, it's much more comfortable to identify up with a male hero than it is for men to identify down to a lower-status [character]."

THOUGH DECONNICK'S COMIC *Captain Marvel* No. 1 immediately sold out when it debuted in 2012, millions of non-comic-reading moviegoers are about to meet her for the first time on the big screen. Directors Anna Boden and Ryan Fleck introduce Carol while she's under the tutelage of an alien warrior (Jude Law) who belongs to the Kree race. At some point, Carol realizes that although she has the powers of a Kree, she is human and had a previous life on Earth that she cannot recall. She visits her home planet to discover her past. While there, she teams up with Samuel L. Jackson's Nick Fury—at this point the future S.H.I.E.L.D. boss is a lowly government desk jockey—to battle the villainous Skrulls, a shape-shifting alien race that has invaded Earth.

The introduction of the dastardly Skrulls means that Boden and Fleck can include cheeky scenes where Carol punches enemies disguised as adorable old grandmas. But their presence could also completely disrupt the Marvel Cinematic Universe: anyone audiences have previously met could be a Skrull in disguise.

Considering that *Captain Marvel* takes place in the 1990s, that leaves decades for the Skrulls to get up to hijinks—and three missing decades for Carol to explain to the Avengers. Where was Captain Marvel when Thanos was collecting Infinity Stones? If she's so powerful, how come none of the Avengers seem to know about her? And how did she prevent herself from aging between the events of *Captain Marvel* and *Endgame*?

What's certain is that the Avengers are counting on Carol to save the day. It took 21 movies for Marvel to put a female superhero at center stage. Now the studio hopes it will take just one film for Captain Marvel to prove herself the most powerful superhero in the universe. □

THE FUTURE OF THE MCU

FOLLOWING *AVENGERS: ENDGAME*, THERE WILL BE A CHANGING OF THE GUARD IN MARVEL MOVIES, INCLUDING GREATER REPRESENTATION OF WOMEN AND PEOPLE OF COLOR

BY ELIANA DOCKTERMAN

COMIC-BOOK SCRIBES CONSTANTLY RECYCLE AND reimagine their characters. The same heroes can survive for decades, even after they die, as they are resurrected in a parallel universe, saved with some elixir or replaced by a new, younger hero. Movies don't have that luxury. Actors age. Their contracts run their course. Their characters' arcs get repetitive.

In 2008, Robert Downey Jr. launched the Marvel Cinematic Universe in *Iron Man*. He has appeared in eight Marvel films since. As *Avengers: Endgame* approaches this spring, the actor has openly hinted that this Marvel movie will be his last. In fact, several fan favorites will probably hang up their capes after the upcoming epic. Chris Evans and Chris Hemsworth—the two other actors who have starred in three solo films and several ensem-

ble pictures—revealed that they have fulfilled their contracts with Marvel Studios.

Marvel hopes the question of whether these three characters will perish or simply retire at the end of that movie is enough to draw millions of moviegoers into theaters. But either way, *Endgame* will mark a pivotal moment in the Marvel Cinematic Universe. Once the original Avengers are gone, Marvel needs new heroes to fuel the next decade of films. The studio has long anticipated the changing of the guard and begun to lay the groundwork for a new superteam. Unlike their predecessors, the new heroes will look more like the diverse, international audience that buys tickets to Marvel movies.

Last year's *Black Panther* began to change the narrative that only white men can be superheroes. Everyone wants to see themselves reflected onscreen,

Black Widow

Black Panther

Spider-Man

Young attendees at a 2018 Black Panther *3-D screening in Nairobi, Kenya, sported cosplay based on the film's characters.*

children especially. Audiences have long clamored for a more diverse array of protagonists at the cinema. Now, 11 years into the MCU, fans will finally get a female solo movie in *Captain Marvel*. A few years down the road, they can expect an Asian superhero film. Marvel is also toying with the idea of bringing a popular Muslim superhero to movie theaters. Such is the studio's bright future.

FOR THE PAST decade, Marvel has relied on a cohort of chisel-jawed white men to propel its films forward. Downey and the three Chrises (Evans as Captain America, Hemsworth as Thor and Pratt as *Guardians of the Galaxy*'s Star-Lord) lead their respective franchises. Even as the studio branched out into more genre-bending fare, like the mystical *Doctor Strange* and the comedic *Ant-Man*, they still featured white male heroes.

Fans have often expressed their frustration with Marvel's lack of diversity. Black Widow fans lobbied for Scarlett Johansson to get her own spinoff. People protested when Marvel whitewashed *Doctor Strange*'s Ancient One by casting a white woman to

play a role written as an Asian man in the comics. Reports have suggested that some studio executives were hesitant to produce more diverse fare for fear of losing their core audience.

Marvel movies lagged behind other major franchises in varying up their principals. *Star Wars* rebooted with three new leads—one female, one black, one Hispanic—and broke box-office records. In 2017, Warner Bros. released *Wonder Woman* four years after rebooting the DC superhero universe—and two years before Captain Marvel would make her big-screen debut.

Black Panther ended the conversation of whether Marvel fans would cheer on heroes who don't look like Captain America. The studio's first solo black superhero film broke dozens of records and became the highest-grossing film in the nation in 2018. "You don't need to look like the hero to relate to them on-screen," Marvel Studios head Kevin Feige told TIME last year. "The success of *Black Panther* has borne that out. As long as it's a great story and told by a master filmmaker, then it will be a success."

In the wake of *Black Panther*, Marvel will celebrate several other "firsts." Its first solo female superhero movie, *Captain Marvel*, is helmed by the directing team of Anna Boden and Ryan Fleck. The studio is billing the part-alien fighter pilot as the most powerful superhero in the entire universe, the person who is expected to swoop in and save the day in *Endgame*. Star Brie Larson has said that she took the role because feminism felt baked into the movie. "There's been so many women involved in the making of it that I don't feel like I've had to fight as much [as I have during the making of other films]," she told Mashable. "I felt understood from the beginning."

Meanwhile, Black Widow is finally getting a spin-off after having toiled as a supporting player in seven Marvel movies. The prequel, to be directed by Cate Shortland, will trace the origin story of Russian spy–turned–S.H.I.E.L.D. agent Natasha Romanoff. Marvel, many fans hope, will continue to introduce female characters so that one woman won't have to represent her entire gender in otherwise all-male ensemble films as Black Widow did in the original *Avengers* and Gamora (Zoe Saldana) did in *Guardians of the Galaxy*. Despite the success of movies such as *Star Wars: The Last Jedi* and *Wonder Woman*, female leads are still hard to come by: a study from San Diego State University's Center for the Study of Women in Television and Film found that women accounted for just 24% of protagonists in the 100 top-grossing domestic films in 2017, the year those aforementioned two movies debuted.

Marvel has also reportedly fast-tracked its first Asian superhero movie. A UCLA report found that Asian characters are among the most underrepresented groups onscreen, accounting for just 3.1% of roles in 2016's top films. No doubt, the massive box-office success of the 2018 rom-com *Crazy Rich Asians* spurred Marvel to push forward with *Shang-Chi*.

Marvel has hired Chinese-American writer Dave Callaham to work on the script, and he will have the chance to either sidestep or interrogate some harmful plotlines from the original comics. The character was originally conceived to capitalize on the success of Bruce Lee's kung fu films in the 1970s, but the story lines often leaned on lazy stereotypes rather than celebrating the character. The treatment of this film is particularly high stakes for Marvel, considering that many fans grew exasperated with the studio's television series *Iron Fist*, about a white male martial artist.

In older franchises like Spider-Man—which will get another solo film this summer—supporting characters could come to the fore. The latest Spider-Man movie, *Homecoming*, even hinted that Miles Morales—a half-black, half–Puerto Rican teen who takes up the Spider-Man mantle in the comic books and the recent animated hit *Spider-Man: Into the Spider-Verse*—could show up in future films.

The only other confirmed project on Marvel's docket is *The Eternals*, an ensemble movie about genetically modified humans. The studio nabbed indie director Chloé Zhao to direct that movie, which has the opportunity to gather a more diverse ensemble cast than Marvel's early films. Feige has also said that he is interested in producing a movie starring Ms. Marvel, the comic-book publisher's first Muslim female superhero.

And then there are the X-Men. Disney and Fox are currently undergoing a merger, which will grant Marvel Studios the rights to famed mutants such as Wolverine and Storm. Those stories have always focused on issues of discrimination—the first X-Men movie literally began in a Nazi concentration camp. It's easy to imagine a diverse cast of X-Men joining the MCU to fight alongside—or perhaps even against—the Avengers.

MARVEL WILL REMAIN tight-lipped about what its next Avengers team will actually look like until *Endgame* rolls its final credits. Teasing many new superheroes would undercut the drama of losing the old ones. But surely a new squad will assemble and Captain Marvel, purported to be Earth and space's mightiest hero, will take a leading role.

Marvel still has a long way to go in terms of representation. The studio has yet to produce a Latinx superhero, a Native American superhero or an openly LGBTQ superhero (though Tessa Thompson took to Twitter to say that her Marvel character, Valkyrie, from *Thor: Ragnarok* is bisexual, even if it wasn't indicated onscreen). And so far, Marvel's planned solo female films feature only white women.

Studios can rarely keep up with the evolving culture: movies takes years to produce, especially multimillion-dollar, CGI-laden epics. But making films that reflect the experiences of the audiences watching them is just good business sense. Time and again, movies like *Black Panther* have proved that if a studio makes a good movie about any superhero, people will flock to see it. □

A TRIP THROUGH THE UNIVERSE

BY EMILY JOSHU

FROM IRON MAN'S ORIGIN TO THANOS'S DECIMATING FINGER SNAP, HIGHLIGHTS FROM AN EPIC CINEMATIC TIMELINE

IRON MAN

RELEASE DATE: MAY 2, 2008
DIRECTOR: JON FAVREAU
BOX OFFICE: $585.2 MILLION

The Marvel Cinematic Universe owes its origin to Tony Stark (Robert Downey Jr.), a "genius, billionaire, playboy philanthropist," as he would later describe himself to a certain group of heroes. Stark is a weapons inventor conducting business overseas when an explosion nearly kills him. Terrorist group the Ten Rings locks him in a cave and demands that he build an advanced missile system. Instead, he builds an arc reactor—an electromagnetic device to be implanted in his chest to keep shrapnel from reaching his heart—and a full-body armored suit. His rival Obadiah Stane (Jeff Bridges) will copy the suit and become Iron Monger.

During the final confrontation with Stane, Stark's assistant Pepper Potts (Gwyneth Paltrow) helps knock Stane out before he crashes to his death in Stark's main arc-reactor facility.

In the final scene, Stark ditches his secret identity and announces at a press conference, "I am Iron Man," before the credits roll.

POST-CREDITS SCENE
In what will become a highly anticipated hallmark of every MCU film, *Iron Man* includes an enigmatic sequence after the final credits have rolled. Here, Tony Stark enters his darkened living room to find a man waiting for him. Stepping out of the darkness, Samuel L. Jackson reveals his identity as Nick Fury, director of S.H.I.E.L.D. "Mr. Stark, you've become part of a bigger universe. You just don't know it yet," he says, adding that he's there to talk about the mysterious Avengers Initiative.

TIME REVIEW
[Director Jon] Favreau . . . lends *Iron Man* the unobtrusive speed and precision of classic comedy. An actor before he was a director, he's not content to let his stars play stereotypes, or even archetypes. Bridges and [Shaun] Toub, and Gwyneth Paltrow as Stark's gal Friday, aren't slumming in the least. They're rising to the material, and elevating it. . . . Downey's the best . . . He sometimes seems to be in his own movie, one that's smarter and faster than the one he's been signed for. But having been entrusted to carry *Iron Man*, Downey sets the pace, establishes the tone and this big movie whirls along to keep up with him. Which it does; it fits Downey as smartly as his Iron Man jumpsuit . . . There's an American style—best displayed in the big, smart, kid-friendly epic—that few other cinemas even aspire to, and none can touch. When it works, as it does here, it rekindles even a cynic's movie love. So cheers to Downey, Favreau and the *Iron Man* production company. They don't call it Marvel for nothing. —*Richard Corliss*

PHASE ONE
THE INCREDIBLE HULK

RELEASE DATE: JUNE 13, 2008
DIRECTOR: LOUIS LETERRIER
BOX OFFICE: $263.4 MILLION

Scientist Bruce Banner (Edward Norton) survives a failed "Super Soldier" experiment involving extreme gamma radiation. The exposure alters his cells and causes him to turn into a green giant known as the Hulk, an affliction of which he desperately wants to rid himself. Fleeing General Thaddeus Ross (William Hurt), the father of Banner's former girlfriend Betty Ross (Liv Tyler), Banner becomes a fugitive and attempts to keep himself from having another "incident" that might transform him into the creature.

Ross assigns special-ops expert Emil Blonsky (Tim Roth) to capture the Hulk. Trying to replicate Banner's condition, Blonsky turns himself into the similar Abomination. In their climactic fight, the Hulk wraps chains around Abomination's throat to strangle him. He has almost killed him when Betty begs him to stop. He complies, showing control over his rage for the first time.

After Banner relocates to a cabin in the mountains of British Columbia, he meditates alone, his pulse rising. Finally able to control the metamorphosis on his own, his pupils turn emerald and he smiles into the camera before the screen goes black.

POST-CREDITS SCENE
A drunken General Ross smokes a cigar at a bar, smelling of "stale beer and defeat," as noted by Tony Stark as he enters. Stark patronizes Ross for the Super Soldier program and tells him that "we" are putting a team together. The scene ends before Stark can answer Ross's question, "Who is 'we?' "

***TIME* REVIEW**
Norton plays Banner a little more soulfully (I think) than Eric Bana did five years ago [in a separate Hulk film], though it doesn't much matter to me that Bruce hates the hulky half of his schizoid personality. All monsters, from Frankenstein's onward, share that feeling and use it to enlist our sympathy. . . . Blonsky morphs into a creature known as the Abomination for purposes of a climactic confrontation with the Hulk that you really don't have to witness since you've seen it in one minor variation or another a dozen times before.

That said, one has to admit that enormous moviemaking skill goes into the creation of pictures like *The Incredible Hulk.* The sheer craft directors such as Leterrier lavish on them is awesome to me. I can't imagine how they orchestrate —or even remember—all the little pieces of film they require to build their big set pieces. That thought, however, is nearly always followed by this question: Why do they bother? —*Richard Schickel*

PHASE ONE

IRON MAN 2

RELEASE DATE: MAY 7, 2010
DIRECTOR: JON FAVREAU
BOX OFFICE: $623.9 MILLION

Several months after revealing his secret identity to the world, Tony Stark is hardly keeping a low profile. Fulfilling the legacy of his father, Howard, he has reopened the Stark Expo convention, to show off his success and confidence just as much as his tech innovations.

However, Stark soon faces the consequences of his new armored persona. The government has launched an investigation into the creation of Iron Man. The palladium fueling his arc reactor has begun to slowly poison him. And the vengeful physicist Ivan Vanko (Mickey Rourke), a.k.a. Whiplash, has joined forces with business mogul Justin Hammer (Sam Rockwell) to vanquish him. With the help of his best friend Lt. Col. James "Rhodey" Rhodes (Don Cheadle, taking over the role from Terrence Howard), a.k.a. the armored hero War Machine, Stark defeats his foes.

At the end of the film, Nick Fury deems Stark a risk and unsuitable for the Avengers Initiative. Or so he thinks.

POST-CREDITS SCENE
In the New Mexico desert, S.H.I.E.L.D. agent Phil Coulson (Clark Gregg) arrives at a remote impact crater where a team has recovered an otherworldly artifact. He makes a phone call, presumably to Nick Fury, saying they found "it"—a large hammer indented in the crater, a clear tease for the MCU's next hero.

PHASE ONE

THOR

RELEASE DATE: MAY 6, 2011
DIRECTOR: KENNETH BRANAGH
BOX OFFICE: $449.3 MILLION

For the first time, the MCU goes beyond Earth by introducing the celestial realm of Asgard, home of Thor, the Norse god of thunder. Just as our hero (Chris Hemsworth) is set to inherit the throne, his father, King Odin (Anthony Hopkins) banishes him to Midgard (a.k.a. Earth) as punishment for his violent response to the Frost Giants of Jotunheim's violating their treaty with Asgard. Thor is also stripped of Mjolnir, the mythical hammer from which his control over thunder and lightning is derived.

Thor's adoptive brother, the god of mischief, Loki (Tom Hiddleston), is the villain of the film (along with Frost Giants king Laufey, played by Colm Feore) and will go on to become one of the MCU's most enduring (and endearing) antagonists. His plan to take over Asgard and conquer Jotunheim is interrupted by the returning Thor, who destroys the Bifrost Portal that connects the various realms, thus preventing Loki's conquests. Loki apparently kills himself by falling off the bridge.

With the portal between worlds destroyed, Thor believes he can no longer return to Earth and longs for the human love interest, scientist Jane Foster (Natalie Portman), he left behind.

***TIME* REVIEW**
The early sequences are clotted with confounding backstory dialogue—like Thor's "Have you forgotten all we've done together?"—that will have non-Marvelettes thinking they've wandered into the middle of another movie. . . . Turns out Branagh has a deft touch after all; he just waits for the modern scenes to reveal it. Evicted from Asgard, Thor lands in the New Mexico desert, getting promptly creamed by astrophysicist and reckless driver Jane Foster (Natalie Portman, in her sixth film released in six months) and tased by her comic sidekick Darcy Lewis (Kat Dennings). A displaced superhero stranded on Earth, where his special gifts are initially inappropriate, Thor acquires some of the clumsy charm of Jeff Bridges's interstellar traveler in *Starman*. —*Richard Corliss*

CAPTAIN AMERICA

THE FIRST AVENGER

RELEASE DATE: JULY 22, 2011
DIRECTOR: JOE JOHNSTON
BOX OFFICE: $370.6 MILLION

Steve Rogers (Chris Evans), a 90-pound underdog, is eager to enlist in the armed forces as the U.S. enters World War II. Rejected by every branch of the military, but exhibiting what scientist Dr. Abraham Erskine (Stanley Tucci) believes is extraordinary courage and conscience, Rogers is recruited for Project Rebirth, a government initiative spearheaded by a young Howard Stark (Dominic Cooper). Administered a secret serum, Rogers is transformed into a supersoldier, a muscular, idealistic military powerhouse—and is christened Captain America.

Facing the looming threat of Hydra, an authoritarian terrorist organization based on Nazi ideals, and its leader, Johann Schmidt, a.k.a. the Red Skull (Hugo Weaving), Rogers becomes what Agent Coulson later refers to as "the world's first superhero."

Following the death of best friend James Buchanan "Bucky" Barnes (Sebastian Stan) during an attack on Hydra, Rogers faces off with Schmidt on board the Red Skull's plane heading to strike the U.S. After defeating Schmidt, Rogers realizes he can't land the aircraft without endangering people, so he redirects the flight path to crash into the Arctic Ocean, sacrificing himself.

Rogers later awakens, only to eventually realize he has been asleep in the ice for nearly 70 years.

POST-CREDITS SCENE
Rogers, who has woken from nearly 70 years in suspended animation, stands with his back to the camera, pummeling a punching bag in an empty gym. Nick Fury emerges, and Rogers asks if he is trying to get him back into the world. "Trying to save it," Fury replies, teeing up the final Phase One film, *The Avengers*.

TIME REVIEW
On its own, *Captain America* is a modestly engaging little-big movie in the median range: well below the first *Iron Man*, somewhat north of *X-Men: First Class*. It approaches one of Marvel's earliest good guys, created in 1941 by writer Joe Simon and illustrator Jack Kirby, with the utmost reverence . . . The only problem is that we've been there—been nearly everywhere Captain America goes—in countless previous movies. The undergrown underdog could be Peter Parker before he became Spider-Man. Steve's skill set isn't so special, since it's served a dozen or more superheroes . . . We get it: G.I. Joe killed Hitler—though, really, it was the Soviet Army that exhausted his troops, and Hitler killed himself.

Other films' handprints are all over *Captain America*. The remarkable visual effects that make the early runty Steve eerily realistic (by superimposing Evans's thinned-out face on a much smaller actor's body) are a refinement on the techniques used to turn Brad Pitt into an old man, a boy and a baby in *The Curious Case of Benjamin Button*. —Richard Corliss

THE AVENGERS

RELEASE DATE: MAY 4, 2012
DIRECTOR: JOSS WHEDON
BOX OFFICE: $1.5 BILLION

In the MCU's much-anticipated first blockbuster crossover, the four solo heroes have come together for Nick Fury's Avengers Initiative: Iron Man, Hulk (now played by Mark Ruffalo), Thor and Captain America. Black Widow (Scarlett Johansson) and Hawkeye (Jeremy Renner) return for much larger roles, taking the last two slots on the roster. Loki uses the Tesseract to power his plans to conquer Earth.

During the climactic "Battle of New York," the Chitauri, Loki's alien allies, invade via an interdimensional portal in the sky. Iron Man redirects a nuclear missile by flying it into the portal to dispatch the threat, but not before the city suffers signification devastation.

Following mixed opinions from the public, the heroes go their own ways, most notably with Thor escorting Loki and the Tesseract back to Asgard. In the final shot, the letters on Stark Tower are gone, with only a hopeful "A" remaining.

POST-CREDITS SCENES
This is the first MCU film with two scenes during the credits. We get our first look at a mysterious purple-skinned alien (whom comics fans recognize as Thanos). His assistant, the Other, seething at Loki's failure to defeat humankind, notes that "to challenge them is to court death." Later, at a New York City shawarma restaurant that was damaged during the battle, the six Avengers eat in exhausted silence.

TIME REVIEW
[Director Joss] Whedon sat on his usual impulse to go meta; instead he served as expert mixologist for this all-star cocktail party. The movie guarantees fast-paced fun without forcing anyone to think about what it all means, which is nothing . . . *The Avengers* doesn't aim for transcendence, only for the juggler's skill of keeping the balls smoothly airborne, and in 3-D too (converted after production). At that it succeeds. . . . And with six superheroes fighting for screen time, the combat sure is as strenuous among them as between them and Loki. Each has a powerful personality, and four of them have starred in their own movies; so a good chunk of *The Avengers* involves the collision of star egos, as if the aircraft carrier were a benefit-concert green room stuffed with celebrities bickering over billing. . . . The new enterprise is just one lavish element in the grand design. With plenty of incident, but limited glimpses into each superhero's soul, the picture falls short of the finest Marvel film, the original *Iron Man*. For all the entertainment value of Whedon's film, the question lingers: Is *The Avengers* too much for one movie, or not enough? —*Richard Corliss*

IRON MAN 3

RELEASE DATE: MAY 3, 2013
DIRECTOR: SHANE BLACK
BOX OFFICE: $1.2 BILLION

Ushering in what Marvel referred to as its second phase of titles, Tony Stark has fallen from peak confidence to unfamiliar vulnerability. Following his near-death experience during the Battle of New York, he shows signs of post-traumatic stress disorder and suffers frequent panic attacks.

With Stark having no time to recover, a new threat emerges. The Mandarin (Ben Kingsley), a mysterious terrorist, launches attacks around the world and directly on Stark's home. But the Mandarin is far from what he seems. He's eventually revealed as an actor meant to distract the public from the true Mandarin, Aldrich Killian (Guy Pearce), a scientist with a vendetta against Stark.

After Stark once again saves the day, he vows that he will give Pepper Potts what she has always wanted: he orders his AI assistant J.A.R.V.I.S (Just A Rather Very Intelligent System) to destroy all of his suits and has the shrapnel and arc reactor removed from his chest.

POST-CREDITS SCENE
Stark lies across a therapist chair, eyes closed, as he reflects on his experiences as Iron Man. He says how nice it is to have someone to share his most intimate thoughts with as the shot expands to reveal Bruce Banner, asleep in the adjacent chair. When Stark asks, "Where did I lose you?" Banner responds with "Elevator in Switzerland"—Stark and Killian's meeting in 1999 in the film's opening scene.

TIME REVIEW
It's a tribute to Downey's gruff charm that he doesn't lose his audience by refusing to sugarcoat Tony's relationship with a winsome boy [who helps him recover from the Mandarin's attack]—and that the most oratorically gifted of current Hollywood stars can turn one word into an aria of self-sufficiency. . . .

Who needs *The Avengers*? Not this movie . . . For all its sprawling diversions, last year's box-office champ seems like small change compared with the much more vigorous and focused *IM3*. Besides rehabbing a hero who overcomes anxiety to save the world and defeat the terror-industrial complex by the simple matter of cloning his body armor, the movie proves that there's still intelligent life on Planet Marvel. As you're propelled out of the theater on *IM3*'s hydraulic lift of pleasures, you're likely to say, "*That* is how it's done." —*Richard Corliss*

PHASE TWO

THOR

THE DARK WORLD

RELEASE DATE: NOV. 8, 2013	
DIRECTOR: ALAN TAYLOR	
BOX OFFICE: $644.6 MILLION	

Having returned to Asgard, the god of thunder must face the ancient Dark Elves, who have unleashed a force called Aether, which makes the Tesseract's power seem minuscule in comparison. When Jane Foster is infected by it, Thor brings her to his world for safety. In the midst of this, Asgard awaits the Convergence, an every-5,000-years event in which the Nine Realms perfectly align.

Meanwhile, bound in shackles, Loki faces life imprisonment for his invasion of Earth. Following the death of his mother, Frigga (Rene Russo), Thor frees his brother from jail and recruits him to help draw Malekith (Christopher Eccleston), leader of the Dark Elves, away from Asgard and rid Foster of the Aether. Loki, however, meets his (apparent) end when Kurse (Adewale Akinnuoye-Agbaje), a lieutenant of Malekith, drives a sword through his body.

Malekith plans to release the Aether on Earth during the Convergence, but with help from Jane and her scientist friends, Thor defeats the Dark Elf. When Thor returns home at the end of the film, Odin agrees to give him the throne. This is not Odin, though; it's an illusion revealed to be trickster Loki.

POST-CREDITS SCENES
Thor's allies Sif and Volstagg meet the spiky-haired, elegant Taneleer Tivan, a.k.a. the Collector (Benicio del Toro), and entrust him with the Aether. Volstagg says the Tesseract is already on Asgard and that it's not wise to keep two Infinity Stones that close together. "One down. Five to go," the Collector says. Later, a flash of light returns Thor to Earth, where he embraces Jane. Elsewhere, a Jotunheim beast, accidentally teleported here, stomps across a parking lot.

TIME **REVIEW**
[Thor] shrivels in character complexity beside Loki, the god of mischief . . . Tom Hiddleston incarnates him as a sinister sylph draped in black leather and chain mail, a Hamlet among hunks . . . Without camping things up, Loki shows that it's *good* to be bad . . . Packing this bulging dramatis personae into a two-hour movie must have been a no-fun chore for its chief assemblers . . . The clutter makes your head feel like it's about to explode—and not in a good way, with wonders upon wonders. Instead it seems like arcana that might show up on the midterm final: the next Marvel movie.

So it's a relief when [Loki] returns to earth to blow stuff up . . . Is this the end of little Loki? We won't say, but do stay seated through the long closing credits, which plant more surprises than the rest of *The Dark World* put together. There you will find an Oscar-winning actor murmuring, "One down. Five to go."

That could refer to a nest of Infinity Stones or to the quintet and more of Marvel sagas. We hope they'll be enlivened by that maleficent spirit, the genius Loki. Long may he rage.
—*Richard Corliss*

CAPTAIN AMERICA

THE WINTER SOLDIER

POST-CREDITS SCENES
Two men, both working for Hydra, meet in a laboratory following the destruction of S.H.I.E.L.D. They have Loki's scepter, which has been infused with the power of the Tesseract. Also in their possession are a pair of super-powered test subjects: a man with super speed and a woman making blocks levitate with her hands. (We'll soon learn they are Quicksilver and Scarlet Witch.) Later, at the Smithsonian's Captain America exhibit, a disguised Bucky stares at his own memorial.

TIME REVIEW

[Rogers's] inborn innocence means he is vulnerable to disillusion; he's constantly learning that the America he was raised to love is a place of compromise and chicanery . . . Evans, an actor who can be just as persuasive playing a serial killer, locates the discomfort of a misfit innocent. [Anthony Mackie] makes a strong debut as the Falcon, who, like Black Widow, deserves his own Marvel movie. Johansson and Redford, together onscreen for the first time since 1998, when she was 15 and he was the Horse Whisperer, enjoy a pointed, prickly reunion. . . . *The Winter Soldier* is no labored treatise on political science; it fulfills all the expectations of a Marvel movie. But this time the danger doesn't emanate from a fantasy villain like Neutron or an imaginary realm like Asgard. It's grounded in threats from today's headlines. (Russia shows up too, though as a victim country—not an invader.) Instead of butter on your movie-theater popcorn, you get a healthy spritz of paranoia. It tastes good. —*Richard Corliss*

RELEASE DATE:	APRIL 4, 2014
DIRECTORS:	ANTHONY RUSSO AND JOE RUSSO
BOX OFFICE:	$714.3 MILLION

Steve Rogers has teamed up with S.H.I.E.L.D. as an agent and befriended former Air Force paratrooper Sam Wilson (Anthony Mackie), who later becomes the flying superhero Falcon. Nick Fury reveals plans for Project Insight, S.H.I.E.L.D.'s response to the increasing concern of international security.

Hydra, which has been infiltrating S.H.I.E.L.D. for decades, has revived and brainwashed Rogers's old friend Bucky Barnes and turned him into their own asset, the Winter Soldier. He attacks Fury, who is presumed dead.

Led by double agent Alexander Pierce (Robert Redford), Hydra intends to take over Project Insight's satellites for nefarious purposes, but Captain America and his allies thwart the threat.

Fury has survived, but with S.H.I.E.L.D.'s reputation tarnished, he goes on the run incognito to uncover the extent of Hydra's mission.

GUARDIANS OF THE GALAXY

RELEASE DATE: AUG. 1, 2014
DIRECTOR: JAMES GUNN
BOX OFFICE: $773.3 MILLION

In 1988, with his mother dying, a young Peter Quill runs out of her hospital room and is captured by a spaceship. Twenty-six years later, Quill (Chris Pratt) has become an outlaw who calls himself Star-Lord. After being arrested, Quill forms an unlikely alliance with fellow inmates Gamora (Zoe Saldana), an assassin; genetically modified raccoon Rocket (Bradley Cooper); humanoid tree Groot (Vin Diesel); and the vengeance-seeking Drax the Destroyer (Dave Bautista). After they escape prison, the five travel the cosmos to ultimately fight the Kree military leader Ronan the Accuser (Lee Pace), powered by an Infinity Stone meant for the alien warlord Thanos (Josh Brolin). The Guardians defeat Ronan, thanks in part to Groot sacrificing himself.

With their criminal records cleared, the group—including a baby version of Groot, growing from his remains—continue their interstellar adventures.

TIME REVIEW

This self-styled "legendary outlaw," unknown to most of his adversaries, is an anomaly in the Marvel canon. The first reel of director-cowriter James Gunn's movie tipped us off that Peter Quill is no Peter Parker, whose guilt over Uncle Ben's death deeply informed his Spider-Man personality. The new Peter, unhaunted and largely conscience-free, is Indy plus Han Solo; and *Guardians* is a jauntier, far brattier *Star Wars*. Alas, making fun and profit of the George Lucas saga is a tactic about 30 years behind the curve; Mel Brooks did it, with giddier panache, in the 1987 *Spaceballs* . . . Peter's gang might be the Wild Bunch of Merry Men— or, more aptly, the far-flung Expendables. For if the Marvel comics owners had held a garage sale of their least valuable subheroes, and you'd bought five, you might have accidentally assembled the Guardians team . . . Something important has to be at stake in a Marvel movie; it isn't here. If the studio bosses think that *Guardians of the Galaxy* has both the weight and the buoyancy that make some Marvel movies supreme entertainments, the joke's on them. —*Richard Corliss*

POST-CREDITS SCENES

Baby Groot dances in his planter to the Jackson 5's "I Want You Back." Later, a metropolitan planet lies in ruins as the injured Collector sits among what's left of his museum. His dog Cosmo, dressed in a space suit, licks his face. "What do you let it lick you like that for?" asks anthropomorphic Howard the Duck, a classic Marvel Comics character created in the 1970s and one of the museum's former residents.

AVENGERS

AGE OF ULTRON

RELEASE DATE: MAY 1, 2015

DIRECTOR: JOSS WHEDON

BOX OFFICE: $1.4 BILLION

The Avengers converge in Sokovia, raiding the base of Hydra head Baron Wolfgang von Strucker (Thomas Kretschmann) to reclaim Loki's scepter. The group capture Strucker but are intercepted by superpowered Sokovian twins Pietro (Aaron Taylor-Johnson) and Wanda Maximoff (Elizabeth Olson), a.k.a. Quicksilver and Scarlet Witch.

Stark and Banner use the scepter to create a secret artificial-intelligence peacekeeping project they name Ultron. However, Ultron (James Spader) suddenly activates on his own, with one goal: eradicating humanity. J.A.R.V.I.S., destroyed by Ultron, is reinvented in physical form as Vision (Paul Bettany) and, along with the Maximoff twins, joins forces with the team.

Ultron's plan culminates in an attack on Sokovia. Pietro is killed in the battle, but Ultron is ultimately defeated when Vision destroys his last remaining drone host.

TIME REVIEW

If anything, [Joss Whedon's] writing is almost too sharp. The characters are so finely drawn and verbally quick . . . that they seem to belong to a different universe than the cartoonish one they find themselves in. They're smarter than it, but in order for the plot to get rolling, Tony Stark has to make the rookie mistake of trying to create a superpowered artificial intelligence using a gem embedded in the staff of Loki, god of evil. You can see Stark actively struggling to convince even himself that this is a good idea. Likewise, no one ever seems quite sure why the nonsuperpowered, merely handy Avengers, Black Widow and Hawkeye are in the group at all, since they're constantly in danger of being squashed like bugs . . . To give the Avengers even a fighting chance, Whedon has to keep Ultron in shackles . . . A real Ultron would be completely distributed and systemic, the way real-life supervillains are: climate change, Ebola, political inertia, economic inequality. You couldn't smash them with Thor's hammer—or you could, but it wouldn't do any good. That would be truly scary. But not nearly as fun to watch.
—Lev Grossman

POST-CREDITS SCENE
A darkened hatch slowly comes into the light, revealing a gold gauntlet. Thanos appears, slipping on the glove, which has six open compartments lining the knuckles. "Fine. I'll do it myself," he says, frustrated by his various intermediaries' failed plans to claim the Infinity Stones.

PHASE TWO

ANT-MAN

RELEASE DATE: JULY 17, 2015
DIRECTOR: PEYTON REED
BOX OFFICE: $519.3 MILLION

Electrical engineer turned burglar Scott Lang (Paul Rudd) has just been released from jail. Jobless and desperate to provide child support for his daughter, Cassie (Abby Ryder Fortson), he accepts a mysterious gig from former cellmate Luis (Michael Peña) to steal an "old motorcycle suit" from former S.H.I.E.L.D. agent Hank Pym (Michael Douglas). Pym, the first Ant-Man, has just been ousted from his company by his own daughter, Hope van Dyne (Evangeline Lilly). After Lang inadvertently triggers an alarm on the suit and shrinks to the size of an insect, Pym tasks him with becoming the next Ant-Man. Their goal is to steal the powerful Yellowjacket suit that Pym's former protégé Darren Cross (Corey Stoll) has created (based on Pym's research) and plans to sell to Hydra.

Ant-Man and Yellowjacket engage in the MCU's most miniature battle to date—literally. They scale down to minuscule form, becoming lost in the sub-atomic Quantum Realm, where Pym believes his wife (and fellow mini-hero the Wasp) is trapped. Cross's suit implodes in the realm and he is killed, but Lang escapes and is ready to rebuild his life.

POST-CREDITS SCENES
Hank reveals to Hope an advanced prototype of a new Wasp suit that he and his wife had worked on but never used—until now. "Maybe it's time we finished it," he says, to which Hope responds, "It's about damn time." Later, Steve Rogers and Sam Wilson have found Bucky Barnes, who has been missing since the end of *Captain America: The Winter Soldier.*

TIME REVIEW
Ant-Man, while based on a minor deity in Marvel's pantheon, is not only one of the more entertainingly human fantasies to come out of the studio, but it also defies the bedrock fanboy aesthetic that you don't want to merely watch the superhero; you want to be the superhero . . . At no time during director Peyton Reed's concoction does a viewer feel he's not being played by a movie that's equal parts revenge tale, redemptive parable, apocalyptic thriller and cornucopia of oedipal clichés. Still, the pace of the wisecracks, pathos, CGI fireworks and scientific double-talk is highly satisfying, even comfortable. Likewise the actors selling it. Rudd has always been a curious quantity, a team player to the point of bench sitting. Likable, popular, he's never gotten the star bump from an Apatow comedy of the kind enjoyed by Steve Carell or Seth Rogen. And in *Ant-Man* once again he's less than the centerpiece, being elbowed aside by the scenery-devouring Michael Douglas . . . Rudd brings the warmth, though, which has never been a Marvel priority. —*John Anderson*

CAPTAIN AMERICA

CIVIL WAR

RELEASE DATE: MAY 6, 2016	
DIRECTORS: ANTHONY RUSSO AND JOE RUSSO	
BOX OFFICE: $1.2 BILLION	

One year after the Sokovia attack, public opinion of the Avengers has become apprehensive and divided. Secretary of State Thaddeus Ross (William Hurt) demands that the Avengers sign the Sokovia Accords, which will establish an international panel meant to keep the team in check. While Tony Stark is supportive of the government intervention, Steve Rogers refuses to sign.

Meanwhile, Sokovian terrorist Helmut Zemo (Daniel Brühl) searches for information regarding Hydra's revival and control of Bucky Barnes. It is later revealed that in 1991 the brainwashed Barnes, under Hydra's command, murdered Stark's parents.

A bombing that kills the king of the African nation Wakanda is pinned on Barnes, which intensifies the team's division. Captain America's allies include Falcon, Hawkeye, Ant-Man and Scarlet Witch, while Iron Man's faction features Black Widow; War Machine; Black Panther (Chadwick Boseman), a.k.a. T'Challa, the heir to the Wakandan throne; and fledgling teenage crime fighter Peter Parker/Spider-Man (Tom Holland). They first battle at a German airport, and the conflict between Captain America and Iron Man culminates in Siberia, where Zemo has lured them. After a spirited tussle, Rogers destroys Stark's suit and leaves with Barnes. Later Cap breaks his allies out of prison.

POST-CREDITS SCENES
Barnes takes refuge in Wakanda, where he's placed in stasis until he can be fully free of his brainwashing. When Rogers says that authorities will come for Barnes if they learn he is there, the new king of Wakanda replies, "Let them try." Later, Parker experiments with the web shooters Stark has made for him.

TIME REVIEW
In *Civil War*, regret feels like progress, a hook of feeling for the actors to grab onto . . . the Russos add enough witty touches to prevent complete brain shutdown: there's Sebastian Stan's beefy, bipolar Bucky Barnes/Winter Soldier handily mounting a spinning motorcycle he's just grabbed out of the air, and the vision of one [hero] standing so tall and mighty above the rest that he could be a Ray Harryhausen stop-motion giant—it's a computer-generated effect that still, somehow, retains enough awkwardness to look endearingly handmade.

Yet *Captain America* is most enjoyable for its quieter moments and for its more intimate special effects, like Scarlet Witch's ability to make tiny tongues of flame leap from fingertip to fingertip, or even just the way Evans's Captain America, frozen in the '40s only to be thawed in a strange, modern world, always looks a little dreamily out of place. . . . And there's a superb new addition, Chadwick Boseman's Black Panther, an African prince turned enigmatic crime fighter. As both man and cat, he's patrician and polished, a touch of class padding quietly onto the scene. Like him, *Civil War*, at its best, is blessedly light on its superhero-booted feet. —*Stephanie Zacharek*

DOCTOR STRANGE

RELEASE DATE: NOV. 4, 2016
DIRECTOR: SCOTT DERRICKSON
BOX OFFICE: $677.7 MILLION

Celebrated yet arrogant neurosurgeon Stephen Strange (Benedict Cumberbatch) narrowly survives a car crash, only to find that his most powerful tools, his hands, are constantly trembling. Fearing the end of his career, Strange obsessively seeks a way to heal himself. Eventually, his quest leads him to Kathmandu, Nepal, after he hears that a sorcerer called the Ancient One (Tilda Swinton) helped a paraplegic man walk again. The Ancient One agrees to train him in the mystic arts.

While educating himself on the Sanctums, three structures that protect Earth, Strange uncovers forbidden texts that teach how to bend time with the Eye of Agamotto amulet. He learns that one of the Ancient One's former students, Kaecilius (Mads Mikkelsen), stole pages from the texts to summon the mystical being Dormammu of the Dark Dimension in order to gain immortality.

Through mastery of the Eye, Strange creates an infinite time loop inside the Dark Dimension and eventually forces Dormammu to leave Earth alone. In the New York Sanctum, Strange abandons his quest for healing and continues his study of the mystic arts.

TIME REVIEW

Doctor Strange has one significant quality that most Marvel adaptations lack: a sense of humor about itself, which it wears as lightly as the most gossamer Cloak of Levitation . . . The streets of New York and Hong Kong fold and unfold like angular M.C. Escher morning glories. Those are great effects the first time you see them, and maybe the second. By the end of *Doctor Strange*, they've been repeated so often that they lose much of their magic. Luckily, the actors retain all of theirs. Although the casting of Scotswoman Swinton as the Ancient One, originally an Asian character, caused some controversy when it was announced, Swinton is so totally weird and out-there that her features and skin color are practically beside the point . . . Cumberbatch, both a natural comedian and a subtle one, knows how to get a big laugh from nothing more than an arched eyebrow. That's got to be one of the biggest and most delicate feats of wizardry in this vast and unknowable universe, and Cumberbatch comes by it effortlessly: no ancient Celtic secret needed. —*Stephanie Zacharek*

POST-CREDITS SCENES

Strange meets with Thor to discuss the threat that Loki poses. Later, Karl Mordo (Chiwetel Ejiofor), the Ancient One's former student who betrays his order at the end of the film, confronts Jonathan Pangborn (Benjamin Bratt), the paraplegic who learned to walk again, and removes his power. "I see at long last what's wrong with the world," Mordo says. "Too many sorcerers."

GUARDIANS OF THE GALAXY

VOL. 2

RELEASE DATE: MAY 5, 2017
DIRECTOR: JAMES GUNN
BOX OFFICE: $863.8 MILLION

Following Ronan's defeat, Peter Quill has finally gained the fame he had desperately sought. When the gang's ship crash-lands on a nearby planet, they are rescued by Ego (Kurt Russell), a being whose planet is an extension of his body. Ego has traveled the galaxy, including to Earth, where he dated Quill's mother, Meredith (Laura Haddock). He reveals that he is Quill's father, but Ego's assistant, Mantis (Pom Klementieff), warns the Guardians of Ego's plan to terraform all the planets where he has children, which will cause their destruction.

Quill nearly dies as he battles Ego, but he is saved by the sacrifice of Yondu (Michael Rooker), leader of the Ravagers, a gang of mercenaries who originally abducted him for Ego. Meanwhile, Gamora and her estranged sister Nebula (Karen Gillan) reconcile over their shared hatred for their father, Thanos.

POST-CREDITS SCENES
Kraglin Obfonteri (Sean Gunn), one of the Ravagers, attempts to control Yondu's Yaka Arrow and inadvertently stabs Drax in the shoulder. Later, Stakar Ogord (Sylvester Stallone) reassembles the Ravagers following Yondu's death. In the third scene, High Priestess Ayesha (Elizabeth Debicki) has created an android-like creature to kill the Guardians. In the fourth scene, teenage Groot is behaving like, well, a teenager: his room's a mess and he's engrossed in video games. Finally, in space, a bored group of alien Watchers walk away from an extremely talkative space-suited informant (Stan Lee).

TIME REVIEW

In the context of modern garden-variety escapist cinema, there's nothing inherently wrong with *Guardians of the Galaxy Vol. 2*, director James Gunn's sequel to his 2014 megahit, both adapted from the Marvel comics series of the same name. But this gag- and plot-stuffed follow-up is also emblematic of all we've come to settle for in movie entertainment: it feels not so much crafted as squirted from a tube. In striving to surprise us every minute with its seen-it-all irony, *Guardians Vol. 2* is actually the surprise-spoiler of all time—our every "Wow!" or "Haha!" has been scripted in advance . . . This is a movie that praises viewers for being cool enough to show up and then proceeds to insult them—but only ironically, see?

Comic-book lore is the closest we have to modern mythology, and so the plot of *Guardians Vol. 2* is packed with conceits that seem monumentally, spiritually important—parables about siblings who don't get along, allegories that speak to our need to slip free of parental control, and the like. —*Stephanie Zacharek*

SPIDER-MAN

HOMECOMING

RELEASE DATE: JULY 7, 2017
DIRECTOR: JON WATTS
BOX OFFICE: $880.2 MILLION

Peter Parker is anxious to become an Avenger, despite Tony Stark's insistence that he's not ready. He focuses that energy on his "Stark Industries Internship"—his local crime-fighting pursuits—and defies Stark's demand that he avoid large-scale villains. He also attempts to act like a normal teenager, pursuing his crush Liz Allan (Laura Harrier) and spending time with best friend Ned Leeds (Jacob Batalon).

Peter's dual identities collide as he comes face-to-face with Adrian Toomes (Michael Keaton), an out-of-work salvager with a vendetta against Stark and the government. He also happens to be Liz's father. Making weapons out of Chitauri technology, Toomes becomes the supervillain the Vulture. Spider-Man, with help from Ned (who has discovered Peter's secret identity), stops Vulture's plan to hijack a government plane filled with weapons.

Finally, Peter gets the offer that he's been waiting for: Stark wants him to become an Avenger. However, he declines, realizing that he would rather be a "friendly neighborhood Spider-Man."

TIME REVIEW

Tom Holland, the young English actor who stars in Jon Watts's likable if sometimes unwieldy *Spider-Man: Homecoming*, is everything Peter Parker/Spider-Man ought to be: charmingly awkward, light on his booted feet, and youthful-looking enough to pass for a high school student . . . He hardly gets hurt, as long as we're not talking about his pride. That buoyant naïveté is key to this *Spider-Man*, and Holland brings it by the jittery bucketful. The movie around him is sometimes glancingly light. Other times it works way too aggressively at being entertainment, rather than just breathing. But Holland, as both Parker and Spidey, is always fun to watch: his bumbling uncertainty and his boyish eagerness make him believable not just as a crime fighter but as a kid . . .

But the real pleasures of *Spider-Man: Homecoming* lie in its quieter moments and in the interplay between the actors. The movie's casting is pure New York, so casually racially mixed that you barely notice it, and once you do, you don't give it a second thought. Why can't more movies be like this?
—*Stephanie Zacharek*

POST-CREDITS SCENES
In prison, Toomes is confronted by another prisoner demanding to know Spider-Man's identity, which he denies knowing. Later, Steve Rogers, in his traditional 1940s Captain America garb, films a PSA on "one of the most valuable traits a soldier or student can have: patience," he says, poking fun at the whole concept of waiting for post-credits scenes. "Sometimes [patience] leads to very little, and it seems like it's not worth it, and you wonder why you waited so long for something so disappointing."

TIME REVIEW

Thor is one of the more ridiculous Marvel superheroes, which also makes him one of the best. You don't need to have multiple generations' worth of superhero mythology under your belt to comprehend this God of Thunder with a hearty appetite for beer and a bodybuilder's brawn; it's permissible to just like him. . . .

Thor: Ragnarok is boyishly eager to reveal Thor's goofy likability to us, as if it were something we hadn't yet cottoned to. Directed by the enormously talented New Zealand filmmaker Taika Waititi, it's well intentioned but ultimately numbing, an instance of fun overkill whose ultimate goal seems to be to put us into a special-effects coma. Not even the occasional inspired touch—like Cate Blanchett as the silky villainess Hela—can save it. It's at least three movies rolled into one, with maybe half a decent one in there . . .

Waititi has a gift for ramshackle madness with a strong undercurrent of compassion—but honestly, where is that going to get you these days?
—*Stephanie Zacharek*

POST-CREDITS SCENES

As Thor and Loki plan a course to Earth, a massive ship appears in their path before the screen goes black. Later, the Grandmaster of Sakaar (Jeff Goldblum), who had earlier held Thor and Loki captive, emerges from an escape hatch into a junkyard and attempts to convince his rebelling subjects that he is on their side.

THOR

RAGNAROK

RELEASE DATE: NOV. 3, 2017
DIRECTOR: TAIKA WAITITI
BOX OFFICE: $854 MILLION

After escaping from the planet Muspelheim—where he is warned that "Ragnarok," the destruction of Asgard, is coming—Thor returns home and learns his father is missing. With Loki, he finds Odin on Earth, in Norway, where he reveals that he's dying. He tells them that Hela (Cate Blanchett), the goddess of death and the sister they never knew existed, will be released from imprisonment upon his death, with the intent to destroy Asgard.

Upon Odin's death, Hela rises and pushes her brothers into retreat in space. Her power continues to grow as she conquers Asgard. Thor and Loki wind up on the planet Sakaar, where they enlist the help of the Hulk and the former Asgardian warrior Valkyrie (Tessa Thompson) to escape. They return home and realize that allowing Ragnarok is the only way to defeat Hela, so they let the Muspelheim ruler Surtur (Clancy Brown) destroy their world. With a ship full of refugees, Thor, now missing an eye as well as his hammer Mjolnir (both thanks to Hela), sets a course for a new home.

PHASE THREE

BLACK PANTHER

RELEASE DATE: FEB. 16, 2018
DIRECTOR: RYAN COOGLER
BOX OFFICE: $1.3 BILLION

Following the death of his father, King T'Chaka (John Kani), in *Captain America: Civil War*, T'Challa returns to Wakanda to take the throne. The African nation prefers to be left alone by the rest of the world, concealing its technological advances and giving the impression that it is a poor farming society.

Erik Stevens (Michael B. Jordan), born in Oakland, Calif., to T'Chaka's brother N'Jobu (Sterling K. Brown), arrives in Wakanda with the body of Ulysses Klaue (Andy Serkis). A black-market arms dealer, Klaue had stolen some of the country's precious and powerful metal vibranium with the help of N'Jobu, who was hoping to expose Wakanda to the world.

Stevens, dubbed Killmonger for his ruthless reputation when serving for U.S. black ops, challenges T'Challa to ritual combat to take the throne. Killmonger wins, and when T'Challa is presumed dead he becomes the new king.

T'Challa is ultimately revived and returns to battle Killmonger, who sustains a critical injury. He refuses an offer of healing from his cousin. "Bury me in the ocean, with my ancestors that jumped from the ships," Killmonger says, "because they knew death was better than bondage."

Later, T'Challa establishes a Wakandan outreach center in Oakland and begins to share his country's secrets with the rest of the world.

POST-CREDITS SCENES
T'Challa addresses the United Nations and promises to share his country's knowledge and resources. "Wakanda will no longer watch from the shadows," he says. "We cannot. We must not. . . . We all know the truth: more connects us than separates us." Later, we learn that Bucky Barnes, a.k.a. the Winter Soldier, has been healed by T'Challa's sister Shuri (Letitia Wright), Wakanda's top technology and science expert.

***TIME* REVIEW**
The only thing wrong with Ryan Coogler's stirring, imaginative *Black Panther* is that in some ways, at least, it's required to fit snugly into the Marvel superhero-movie mold. What would this film have been like if its action scenes had been cut cleanly and clearly, instead of chopped into the usual wasteful, visually confusing slice-and-dice mashup? The whole thing moves a little too fast: there are so many gorgeous details—from Ruth E. Carter's Afro-futurist costumes to Hannah Beachler's Emerald City-a-go-go production design—that you might find yourself wishing you could linger on certain images just a bit longer.

But *Black Panther* is still a cut above—perhaps many cuts above—any other recent superhero movie, and some not-so-recent ones too . . . The movie is smart, lavish and fun without being assaultive. —*Stephanie Zacharek*

AVENGERS
INFINITY WAR

RELEASE DATE: APRIL 27, 2018
DIRECTORS: ANTHONY RUSSO AND JOE RUSSO
BOX OFFICE: $2 BILLION

After 10 years of set-up, this installment is the equivalent of an MCU all-star game. Picking up from *Thor: Ragnarok*, the Asgardian refugee ship has been attacked by Thanos (Josh Brolin), who is searching for the Infinity Stones. He kills Loki in order to obtain the Space Stone (housed in the Tesseract).

On Earth, Doctor Strange and Iron Man battle Thanos's deputies and, with Spider-Man's help, save the Time Stone. In space, the Guardians of the Galaxy rescue Thor, and soon several teams are working to save the remaining stones, which Thanos will use to complete the Infinity Gauntlet and cut the universe's population in half. (His motivation: the destruction of his home planet due to overpopulation.)

The outlook is grim. Thanos brutally continues collecting the stones, including murdering his daughter Gamora to obtain the Soul Stone. Strange goes through millions of possible scenarios and discovers that there is only one way to defeat the Mad Titan.

In Wakanda, a group of Avengers joins forces with Black Panther's army to battle Thanos's soldiers. But ultimately Thanos collects all of the stones, and with a snap of his fingers his plan goes into effect: several characters spontaneously turn to dust, including Black Panther, Doctor Strange, Spider-Man, Star-Lord, Scarlet Witch, Falcon and Bucky Barnes. Notably surviving are most of the original Avengers, who now must figure out a way to stop Thanos.

POST-CREDITS SCENE
Nick Fury and S.H.I.E.L.D. agent Maria Hill (Cobie Smulders) are among the people who disintegrate, but not before Fury transmits a mysterious distress call. After he disappears, we see that he sent the signal to a screen with a red, blue and gold symbol that comic-book fans recognize as the crest of Captain Marvel.

TIME REVIEW

There's no pacing in *Avengers: Infinity War*. It's all sensation and no pulse. Everything is big, all of the time . . . There's potential poetry buried deep in [this film]. But it's not a sturdy enough crocus to push through the movie's ironclad surface. There is at least one truly poignant idea here: Thanos's goal of destroying half the universe is much worse than pulverizing the whole thing, because those who remain will remember the world as it was—and they'll be left to mourn those who are gone. The movie's climax scratches at something close to melancholic grandeur, featuring a visual effect that's biblical in both its force and its delicacy. But it's way too little too late. *Avengers: Infinity War* knows what a big deal it is. Just about all the Avengers together, in one two-hour-and-40-minute movie, battling the most power-mad villain there ever was: Wow! Better not blow this one. And so the movie treats audience expectations like a set of ice-cube trays to be filled, and in the end, you have to admit it's very thorough. That's not the nicest thing you can say about it; it's the most damning. —*Stephanie Zacharek*

ANT-MAN AND THE WASP

RELEASE DATE: JULY 6, 2018
DIRECTOR: PEYTON REED
BOX OFFICE: $622.7 MILLION

Scott Lang has been forced into house arrest after his involvement with Captain America's breakaway squad in *Civil War*. Hank Pym and Hope van Dyne, also under governmental fire for providing Lang with his Ant-Man technology, have cut all ties with him. They continue to research the Quantum Realm, where they believe Hank's wife and Hope's mother, Janet van Dyne (Michelle Pfeiffer), has been trapped for 30 years. They kidnap Lang to help them, and Hope suits up as the Wasp in a winged supersuit that allows her to shrink and shoot energy blasts.

Standing in their way is Ava Starr (Hannah John-Kamen), a.k.a. Ghost, whose body has become unstable from a quantum experiment that killed her parents when she was a child. Her plans could put Janet in jeopardy.

Following a series of capers and breakouts, they rescue Janet, and she helps stabilize Ava's condition. As the film ends, Scott is finally released from house arrest.

POST-CREDITS SCENES
While Scott is in the Quantum Realm collecting energy, Hank, Hope and Janet turn to dust as part of Thanos's *Infinity War* finger snap. Later, one of Lang's giant "pet" ants plays the drums in his apartment as an emergency broadcast signal plays on the TV screen.

TIME **REVIEW**

There's no phony nihilist world destruction, no apocalyptic overkill. It's all just Ant-Man—and, this time around, his lithe, nervy winged partner, Wasp, played by Evangeline Lilly—shrinking down, growing big and returning to normal size, over and over. Tiny, big, normal. Tiny, big, normal. As Prince once said, there's joy in repetition.

It was great fun the first time around . . . But *Ant-Man and the Wasp* . . . has to live up to the same daunting, teeny-tiny stakes: it has to be more of the same, but better, and the movie doesn't quite succeed. You can't really make a bigger, better *Ant-Man*—that just means defying the diminutive, carefree scale that made the earlier movie work in the first place. . . .

The movie's best moments are at the beginning, when Scott, trapped at home, gets to spend some quality time with his daughter, Cassie . . . In that sense, *Ant-Man and the Wasp* reinforces the classic Christmas-morning phenomenon: sometimes the big fancy toy isn't nearly as much fun to play with as the plain box it came in. —*Stephanie Zacharek*

HOW WELL DO YOU KNOW THE MCU?

1. True or False: Iron Man has appeared in more MCU films than Captain America.

2. Which actor has not played the Hulk/Bruce Banner?

A. Eric Bana
B. Mark Ruffalo
C. Henry Cavill
D. Edward Norton

3. Which of these is not one of Stan Lee's MCU cameo roles?

A. Mental-institution patient
B. High school science teacher
C. Smithsonian security guard
D. Larry King

4. What is Black Widow's real name?

A. Hope van Dyne
B. Wanda Maximoff
C. Peggy Carter
D. Natasha Romanoff

5. Thanos first appeared in a post-credit scene of which film?

A. *Thor: The Dark World*
B. *Guardians of the Galaxy*
C. *Iron Man 2*
D. *The Avengers*

6. In which of these movies does Loki not meet his (apparent) death?

A. *Thor*
B. *The Avengers*
C. *Thor: The Dark World*
D. *Avengers: Infinity War*

7. True or False: The same actor who voiced J.A.R.V.I.S. also plays Vision.

8. True or False: Benedict Cumberbatch plays more than one role in *Doctor Strange*.

9. What is the name of *Black Panther*'s all-female special-forces squad?

A. Wakanda Warriors
B. Valkyries
C. Jabari
D. Dora Milaje

10. Which of these directors did not have an acting role in his film?

A. Kenneth Branagh, *Thor*
B. Jon Favreau, *Iron Man*
C. James Gunn, *Guardians of the Galaxy*
D. Taika Waititi, *Thor: Ragnarok*

11. What is the name of Star-Lord's ship in *Guardians of the Galaxy*?

A. Hasselhoff
B. Celestial
C. Milano
D. Statesman

12. True or False: The airport battle in *Captain America: Civil War* is set in Austria.

13. Which of these Marvel TV shows is not set in the MCU?

A. *Agents of S.H.I.E.L.D.*
B. *The Gifted*
C. *Daredevil*
D. *The Punisher*

14. Which is the final Infinity Stone that Thanos adds to his gauntlet?

A. Power Stone
B. Soul Stone
C. Mind Stone
D. Reality Stone

15. True or False: *Black Panther* is the first MCU film to earn a Golden Globes nomination for best picture.

OUTSIDE OF THE MCU

SOME OF MARVEL'S EARLIEST COMIC-BOOK CREATIONS (THE X-MEN, SPIDER-MAN, THE FANTASTIC FOUR) INITIALLY MADE THEIR WAY TO THE SCREEN AS SELF-CONTAINED FRANCHISES NOT WITHIN THE UNIVERSE

BY EMILY JOSHU

CAPTAIN AMERICA AND THE HUMAN TORCH MAY look oddly familiar to moviegoers, but not to their respective teammates. Chris Evans has played both characters, creating an amusing paradox that has existed in Marvel films in the 21st century. Outside of the Marvel Cinematic Universe—in which Evans's Captain America has for years saved the world solo and alongside the Avengers—there exists a group of self-contained franchises. That includes the *Fantastic Four* movies, in which Evans played Johnny Storm, a.k.a. the Human Torch, in the first two adaptations. (In the third, Michael B. Jordan took over the role, a few years before he was cast as Erik Killmonger in the MCU's *Black Panther*.)

Also living outside the MCU are the *X-Men* films (including spinoffs featuring Hugh Jackman's Wolverine), the *Deadpool* movies, the first two *Spider-Man* series, the original *Hulk* and a few other assorted properties. Although these characters have shared an interconnected world on the pages of Marvel's comics since the 1960s, they followed distinct roads to the big screen.

LICENSES TO THRILL

THE ORIGINS OF THIS DISPARATE SLATE CAN BE traced to the bankruptcy that Marvel fell into in 1996. The company used licensing deals to help get back on its feet, selling the rights to the X-Men, the Fantastic Four and Daredevil to 20th Century Fox, Spider-Man to Sony and the Hulk to Universal. These early Marvel movies helped launch the modern superhero movement, attracting audiences beyond diehard comic-book lovers. The first, 2000's *X-Men*, earned $296 million at the worldwide box

X-Men *(2000)*

Fantastic Four *(2005)*

Spider-Man 2 *(2004)*

office, and *Spider-Man* took home a staggering $821 million two years later.

By the time the MCU was launched in 2008 with *Iron Man*, the X-Men universe had already created a complex mythology. To date, there have been nine movies featuring the beloved mutants, including prequels, sequels and spinoffs. That doesn't include the two *Deadpool* movies, which exist loosely in this world, or the upcoming *Dark Phoenix*, featuring Sophie Turner's version of Jean Grey based on an iconic comic-book story line.

Although the X-Men films and the MCU have no overlap, they do share a character, the super-speedster Quicksilver. In 2014's *X-Men: Days of Future Past*, his name was Peter (the son of the villain Magneto), and he was played by Evan Peters. The following year, in *Avengers: Age of Ultron*, he was Pietro (portrayed by Aaron Taylor-Johnson), and he wasn't labeled as a "mutant," since that distinction is strictly X-Men domain. (It's possible we may soon see actual crossover. With Disney, which owns Marvel, acquiring Fox, the X-Men could potentially join the MCU. "The notion of the characters coming back is great," Marvel Stu-

dios boss Kevin Feige told *Variety* in December. "It's nice when a company that created all these characters can have access to all those characters.")

The X-Men franchise took a grim turn with 2017's *Logan*, a tale of Wolverine's final days in the year 2029. The film showed an older, grislier and more tired Logan caring for a young girl, Laura (Dafne Keen), with abilities similar to his own, giving the series a much darker energy. TIME critic Stephanie Zacharek noted the "bleak nihilism" at the time of its release, stating that "there's no doubt that *Logan*, with its focus on persecuted outsiders, is tapping the national mood of at least half the country right now." The screenplay earned an Oscar nomination for writers Scott Frank, James Mangold and Michael Green.

SPIDER-MAN'S TANGLED WEB

ARGUABLY MARVEL'S MOST POPULAR SUPERHERO, Spider-Man followed quickly on the heels of the X-Men. His first self-titled film, released by Sony in 2002, brought lanky, awkward teen Peter Parker (Tobey Maguire) to life in what TIME critic Richard Corliss predicted would start a movement. "In emphasizing angst over energy, the movie is much like its hero—not the dashing crime fighter in a red-and-black bodysuit but the introspective nerd who both endears and exasperates," he wrote. "Just as Peter's transformation is a process of trial and error, so the series may be able to mature in the planned sequels."

He was right. The series' success only grew with 2004's *Spider-Man 2*. Director Sam Raimi pulled the rare feat of making a sequel that improved on his original. "Now this is what a superhero movie should be," raved critic Roger Ebert, who singled out the story's emphasis on Peter Parker rather than his alter ego. "The movie demonstrates what's wrong with a lot of other superhero epics: they focus on the superpowers and short-change the humans behind them."

After a third film in 2007, Sony decided it was time for a change and went back to the beginning with a new actor (Andrew Garfield) and a tweaked origin story. But in a sign that moviegoers might have been experiencing Spider-Man fatigue, the two films in this reboot, *The Amazing Spider-Man* (2012) and *The Amazing Spider-Man 2* (2014), fell short of expectations, both critically and commercially.

For the next incarnation, Marvel Studios brokered a deal with Sony to finally bring the character into the MCU. Tom Holland donned the costume for an appearance in *Captain America: Civil War* before headlining his own movie in 2017, the wildly popular *Spider-Man: Homecoming*. A sequel, *Far from Home*, is set to be released in the summer of 2019.

NOT SO FANTASTIC

DESPITE THE FANTASTIC FOUR'S PEDIGREE AS THE characters who began Marvel's comic-book revolution in the 1960s, their onscreen exploits have underwhelmed. The team made its cinematic debut in 2005 under director Tim Story and starring Ioan Gruffudd, Jessica Alba and Michael Chiklis, along with Evans, and the response was far from fantastic. Ebert called the movie "all setup and demonstration, and naming and discussing and demonstrating, and it never digests the complications of the Fantastic Four and gets on to telling a compelling story." A 2007 sequel didn't do much better, and when Fox rebooted the franchise in 2015 with director Josh Trank and a new cast (including Jordan), it received a dismal 9% approval rating on Rotten Tomatoes.

Before he was a member of the Avengers, the Incredible Hulk had his own showcase in 2003. Eric Bana starred as Bruce Banner, while his gamma-radiated alter ego was computer generated. Some critics praised director Ang Lee's more cerebral take on the genre. "The worst thing I can say about this movie is that it's so smart, so deep, so well done, it might be too good for the teenage-boy audience these films are usually aimed at," noted *Good Morning America*'s Joel Siegel. "Then again, that might be the best thing I can say about it."

Marvel soon regained the film rights to the character from Universal and brought him into the nascent MCU in 2008 with a new incarnation, starring Edward Norton. Despite a relatively positive response, Marvel Studios opted not to produce any other solo films for the green goliath, instead weaving the character—now played by Mark Ruffalo—throughout its other movies.

Daredevil, another popular comic-book hero, had a short big-screen life span, following an unsuccessful 2003 version starring Ben Affleck. (The character earned his redemption with a well-received solo TV series that ran for three seasons on Netflix and was considered to be part of the MCU.)

The ability of lesser-known Marvel characters to succeed at the box office was proved once again in 2016's *Deadpool*. The raunchy, R-rated film was praised largely for the self-aware portrayal by Ryan Reynolds, who "delivers every line with a smirk you can hear," Stephanie Zacharek wrote. The character frequently smashes through the fourth wall, addressing the audience with his own commentary and acknowledging the ridiculousness of his adventures. According to Zacharek, he's "the Marvel character for people who think they're too smart for comic books but read them anyway." A lot of people who don't read comics also hit the theaters: *Deadpool* and its 2018 sequel together earned more than $1.5 billion worldwide.

The most recent live-action non-MCU film was *Venom*, a surprise box-office hit last fall, earning more than $800 million worldwide. Reviews were generally mixed, with Zacharek writing that "*Venom* has energy, style and Tom Hardy—all good things. But it doesn't really make sense, a bad thing." Hardy played Eddie Brock, a TV journalist who becomes host to the titular alien symbiote, in the Sony production, which was not directly connected to the MCU. Although the character is a Spider-Man nemesis in the comics, the wall crawler wasn't mentioned in the film. But given the movie's success, it's possible Venom could eventually appear in the MCU. Only time—and evolving licensing deals—will tell. □

SPIDER-MAN'S STICKING POWER

BY ELIANA DOCKTERMAN

YOUR FRIENDLY NEIGHBORHOOD SPIDER-MAN—who, despite his modest moniker, has starred in no fewer than eight live-action movies in 17 years—has become the most overexposed superhero of all. In 2018 alone, the webslinger starred in three huge projects: *Infinity War,* the *Spider-Man* video game and an animated film called *Spider-Man: Into the Spider-Verse.* And yet all three were met with widespread acclaim and commercial success. That list excludes *Venom,* an offbeat film about Spider-Man's villainous doppelgänger, and even that was a box-office smash. The character's proliferation presents the question: Why aren't audiences sick of Spidey?

Marvel legends Stan Lee and Steve Ditko conceived Spider-Man in 1962, when impressive but inaccessible heroes dominated comic books: Superman was an alien, Wonder Woman a demigoddess, Batman a brooding billionaire. Peter Parker was just a nerdy high school kid who couldn't work up the courage to ask out the girl next door. He was young—like his audience—funny, flawed and relatable.

Spider-Man may be Marvel's most popular character, but his success on the big screen has never been a guarantee. Following Sam Raimi's acclaimed trilogy starring Tobey Maguire, Sony rebooted the series with two middling films starring Andrew Garfield that retreaded the ground of their predecessors. After all, an audience can be asked only so many times to watch Uncle Ben die while muttering something about power and responsibility.

And yet Sony has found a way to evolve a well-worn origin story. Another reboot in 2017, aptly called *Spider-Man: Homecoming,* revived Spidey's film career. Like the two versions that came before, the story centered on a young, awkward white guy. But for the first time, Peter's diverse group of friends realistically reflected the population of Queens, N.Y.

The 2018 PlayStation video game *Marvel's Spider-Man* inched closer to modern reality too: in that version of the story, Peter is eight years into his career as a superhero and dealing with adult problems, like how he and Mary Jane—who is now a journalist rather than an aspiring actor—can combat the dated gender roles of hero and damsel in order to fight evil as a team.

But *Into the Spider-Verse,* which won the Golden Globe Award for best animated motion picture, finally asked the most interesting question: What if that pesky arachnid had bitten someone else as well? The movie details the origin story of Miles Morales (voiced by Shameik Moore), the teenage son of a black policeman (Brian Tyree Henry) and a Puerto Rican nurse (Luna Lauren Velez). Created by Brian Michael Bendis and Sara Pichelli, Miles has patrolled the streets of New York City for years in the comics, but his big-screen debut thrust him into the larger pop-culture conversation.

The film asserts that there's nothing particularly special about Peter Parker, which may sound like sacrilege to comic-book purists. It begins with a cheeky montage of Peter's life, including the em-

Into the Spider-Verse—*featuring Peter B. Parker, Gwen Stacy and Miles Morales—mixed computer animation with hand-drawn art and comic-book-influenced design.*

anyone—can wear the mask.

For Sony, that means an endless number of sequel and spinoff possibilities: the studio has already green-lighted *Spider-Verse 2* and a Gwen Stacy movie. For audiences, especially kids, the multitude of heroes offers the reassuring message that you don't have to be a white dude to save the world.

Anyone already overwhelmed by the number of Spider-People onscreen should ready themselves: Tom Holland will star in *Avengers: Endgame* as well as another solo film, *Far from Home*. Meanwhile, Sony is expanding the world of Spider-Man heroes and villains ever further with a *Venom* sequel, a Black Cat solo film and a movie about the villainous vampire Morbius.

Miles won't be relegated to animated films forever, either: he plays a key role in the PlayStation game, and the end teases an expanded Miles story line in the inevitable sequel. Even the Holland films have hinted at Miles's eventual appearance in the live-action movies. The question is whether Sony can maintain Miles's appeal. The studio misstepped when Peter's powers turned him into a cocky hero in the Garfield films. Any Spider-Man or Spider-Woman should feel overwhelmed by the responsibility.

At a time when characters such as Wonder Woman and Black Panther have become icons of strength—they're literally a deity and a king—Spider-Man reminds audiences of just how vulnerable heroes can be. The best moments from the Spider-Man canon are those that zero in on Peter's youth and innocence: that time when a trainful of New Yorkers save a maskless Spider-Man in *Spider-Man 2* and realize their hero is only a teen; the much-memed moment in *Infinity War* when Spider-Man mumbles, "Mr. Stark, I don't feel so good," like a little kid; and, in *Into the Spider-Verse,* a scene in which Miles rips off his own mask to reveal to an enemy that he's just some terrified high schooler.

As long as Spidey is a vulnerable hero, what the person under the mask looks like isn't all that important. *Spider-Verse* does not make much hay of the gender or ethnicity of Miles, Gwen or Peni. What matters is that they each remind audiences that, to quote Aunt May, "There's a hero in all of us." □

barrassing emo dance sequence from *Spider-Man 3* and a Christmas album. "I always find a way to come back," Peter says, winking at his unusual resilience. And then, as Miles looks on, Peter dies—at the hands of the villain Kingpin (Liev Schreiber), who opens a hole in the space-time continuum, ushering several other Spider-People from alternate universes into Miles's Brooklyn.

First comes a curmudgeonly, 40-year-old Peter B. Parker (Jake Johnson), who's divorced, a little chubby and very jaded. (Miles moans, "Why did I get stuck with the janky, old, broke hobo Spider-Man?") But this Peter reluctantly mentors Miles, and later the two join forces with their spidery siblings from other worlds—Gwen Stacy (Spider-Woman, played by Hailee Steinfeld), a black-and-white Peter Parker (Spider-Man Noir, voiced by Nicolas Cage), an anime-inspired Peni Parker (Kimiko Glenn) and a pig named Peter Porker (John Mulaney as Spider-Ham). The movie suggests that anyone—no, really,

THE EVOLUTION HAS BEEN TELEVISED

FROM EARLY ANIMATION TO TODAY'S DYNAMIC LIVE-ACTION DRAMAS, MARVEL HAS A LONG AND COLORFUL HISTORY OF BRINGING ITS HEROES TO LIFE ON TV

BY MARISA ROFFMAN

DECADES BEFORE MARVEL TOOK THE WORLD BY storm with films starring the X-Men, Spider-Man and the Avengers, many of its beloved characters made their first leaps off the page onto the small screen.

The inaugural show, 1966's *The Marvel Super Heroes*, was an animated anthology that ran in syndication, featuring Captain America, Iron Man, Thor, the Hulk and the Sub-Mariner; it drew inspiration directly from the comics for its stories. Spider-Man got his own solo showcase—and a catchy theme song ("Spider-Man, Spider-Man, does whatever a spider can . . .")—in a self-titled series that ran from 1967 to 1970. Over the years, multiple cartoon takes on the Fantastic Four and the Hulk followed, in addition to series starring the Silver Surfer and Iron Man.

But arguably the defining animated Marvel creation was the five-year run of *X-Men* on Fox Kids in the '90s. The show, which included the team-up of Wolverine, Storm, Jean Grey, Cyclops and Professor X, proved to be a commercial hit and pushed the boundaries of what was expected from a series geared toward a younger audience. "Our show demonstrated that the Marvel universe, as a whole, had commercial value far beyond what anybody estimated," Will Meugniot, an artist and producer on the series, told the *Hollywood Reporter* in 2017.

Added Sidney Iwanter, a former Fox Kids executive: "Serialized storytelling had never been attempted before on Saturday morning [at this level]. A story arc that extends over weeks adds all sorts of new wrinkles to the mix." Defying the conventional wisdom of TV programmers, young viewers were

Following two 1977 TV movies, The Incredible Hulk ran for 80 episodes between 1978 and '82. Three reunion movies aired from 1988 to '90.

Spider-Man (1967–70)

not deterred by the ongoing plot or by episodes that ended without a clear resolution.

THE RESULTS WERE mixed for the live-action adaptations in the 1970s. The two-season *Amazing Spider-Man* series starring Nicholas Hammond on CBS was a disappointment. "There was no heart to the series," Marvel's Stan Lee explained in the documentary *With Great Power: The Stan Lee Story*. "A villain would be doing something, and he'd become Spider-Man and go chase the villain and catch him and climb up a building, and that was it. And after the first few episodes, I realized it was going to go nowhere . . . Luckily, it didn't ruin the character for other things." Lee was correct: it was just one of a dozen shows set in the Spider-verse over the years.

The Incredible Hulk, however, was a success by remaining truer to the comic-book character while also knowing when to adapt to its new medium. The CBS series, starring Bill Bixby as Dr. David Bruce Banner and Lou Ferrigno as Banner's anger-fueled (green) persona, ran from 1977 to 1982 and led to three follow-up TV movies. "[Executive producer] Ken Johnson . . . made it an intelligent, adult show that kids could enjoy," Lee told IGN in 2000. "He

took a comic-book character and made him somewhat plausible. . . . He changed it quite a bit from the comic book, but every change he made made sense." One of the biggest tweaks was not having the Hulk speak, as opposed to his primitive "Hulk smash!" bellowing from the comics. "That would have been corny as hell on the screen," Lee admitted. "If you remember the Hulk series, you only really saw the Hulk for about five minutes in an hour show . . . It was a real, great, suspenseful, adult show with enough of the Hulk to please the young kids."

Though a few more live-action shows were attempted, Marvel only got serious about moving into television in 2010. Jeph Loeb, who had experience in both the comics industry and television production, was tapped to lead the charge. There were stop-starts with its planned first projects—including a 2010 attempt at Jessica Jones at ABC that fell through—before *Marvel's Agents of S.H.I.E.L.D.* was officially ordered for the 2013–14 season.

The ABC series had an instant tie to the Marvel Cinematic Universe, centering on Phil Coulson (Clark Gregg), an agent of the Strategic Homeland Intervention, Enforcement and Logistics Division. Coulson, a fan favorite, had previously been one of

X-Men (1992–97)

Agents of S.H.I.E.L.D. (2013–present)

the through-lines for the early MCU films. But his presence also guaranteed a built-in mystery for the show: Coulson was seemingly killed off in 2012's *The Avengers*.

"I remember working through my many stages of grief and saying goodbye to the wonderful Phil Coulson," Gregg admits. But *S.H.I.E.L.D.* co-creator (and *Avengers* director) Joss Whedon and Loeb came to him with the idea that perhaps Coulson wasn't as dead as it originally appeared; now he would be heading up his own team of agents who were coping with a super-powered world. "The whole first season was a mystery, with him trying to figure out what was going on with him," Gregg recalls. "I thought that was an amazing idea, a great mythology, and that got me really excited."

The first season of *Agents of S.H.I.E.L.D.* had "birth pangs," Gregg acknowledges, as the series couldn't initially reveal—until after *Captain America: The Winter Soldier* was released in April 2014— that Hydra had infiltrated S.H.I.E.L.D. decades earlier. And there was the added pressure of being the first show from the new Marvel Television division. "I would pop in and out of Marvel movies . . . be the snarky comic relief from time to time," Gregg

says. "Suddenly, he was the head of a team of new agents doing something new in *S.H.I.E.L.D.* They were dealing with the world as it had been rebooted post–*Avengers*' alien-superhero reveal. Similarly, I was with a new team, trying to do something that hadn't been done before—bring the Marvel story-telling, the Marvel world, to network television. We had a very mirror experience . . . It felt equally as perilous as the adventures we were acting."

The show survived the early bumpy road and thrived. In addition to crossing the 100-episode milestone in 2018, the drama airs its sixth season in 2019, and a seventh season has already been ordered. And *S.H.I.E.L.D.* led to *Agent Carter* (starring Hayley Atwell, who reprised her memorable MCU role of Peggy Carter), which ran for two seasons on ABC.

Though there remain ties between the film and live-action-television worlds—"It's all connected" is the often-repeated mantra—the overlap has decreased as the number of shows Marvel is developing has expanded. "It's important to us that our characters do exist in a singular universe," Loeb says. "We're very open with coordinating with each other, because we have so many series that

Daredevil *(2015–18)*

Jessica Jones *(2015–present)*

are actively going on."

The current animated world on Disney XD maintains its own strong connection, as *Marvel's Avengers Assemble* (which kicked off a Black Panther arc in 2018) and *Marvel's Guardians of the Galaxy* co-exist with overlapping characters.

IN 2013, THE television division set the path for its own expanded universe that would build to a crossover. Netflix ordered individual series *Daredevil* (with the first season released in 2015), *Jessica Jones* (2015), *Luke Cage* (2016) and *Iron Fist* (2017), as well as the team-up season, *The Defenders* (2017). It was a risk, at least on paper. At the time, the streaming platform had just started up its original programming. But "to have something like *Daredevil* come on, it was like, 'What is this?'" Loeb recalls. "Then we followed it up with *Jessica Jones*, who is really a character not many people knew about. And it talked about things that were unexpected for what people would classify as a superhero show. It blew the lid off of where you could go." Indeed, Netflix's take on Jones, a private investigator with super strength, dealt with topics like post-traumatic stress disorder and addiction—and

scored the series a Peabody Award in 2016.

Marvel continued its TV expansion in 2017, launching six new live-action shows: *Legion* (FX) and *The Gifted* (Fox), which are loosely set in the X-Men's super-powered mutant universe; *Inhumans* (ABC); *The Punisher* and the aforementioned *The Defenders* (Netflix); and *Runaways* (Hulu), about a group of teens trying to take down their villainous parents. (It also debuted three animated properties: *Marvel Future Avengers*, *Marvel's Spider-Man* and *Big Hero 6: The Series*.)

"What we've managed to do is put different shows in boxes," Loeb explains. "The first is the Marvel heroes, and those are the series that most directly involve themselves with the movies. And then there are characters we refer to as the street-level heroes [often found on Netflix, which we've dubbed] Marvel Knights. These are the heroes that are much more interested in saving the streets, sometimes saving themselves. And they tend to be much more personal stories and much more insular stories about our characters."

"And then [in 2017], we knew that Tom Holland was going to be playing Spider-Man [in the MCU films]," he continues. "We looked at that and said,

Legion (2017–present)

young heroes are something that works really well on television. And it's a space that's not occupied." Loeb drew on his previous experience working on *Smallville*, which followed a young Clark Kent dealing with teenage angst. "Coming up with young heroes was something that excited us a lot. That's where *Runaways* on Hulu and [2018's] *Cloak & Dagger* on Freeform came along."

The growth has not been unstoppable, however. Netflix canceled most of its Marvel lineup in 2018, leaving only the upcoming season of *Jessica Jones* on its slate.

OCCASIONALLY, SOMETHING POPS up that falls outside of Marvel's pre-established framework. "Whenever it happens, it invigorates the company," Loeb says. "We now have a whole new playground to work in." One such show was *Legion*, crafted by *Fargo* executive producer Noah Hawley. With Fox owning the rights to the X-Men characters at the time of the show's conception, FX boss John Landgraf approached Marvel about Hawley's idea for the series. Although Marvel had taken swings in the past with its shows, nothing was quite as large as this: the telepathically powered David Haller

(*Downton Abbey* alum Dan Stevens)—also known as Legion, the son of Professor X—was an unreliable narrator, in a series full of surreal elements.

"Noah had a unique take on a practically unknown character within the Marvel universe," Loeb says. "It was all in the very first pitch. He started with 'I don't know how many of you know what it means to tell a story in surreal terms.' We don't usually get that when talking about *Luke Cage* or *Runaways*. This was a storyteller who was making clear if we were going to do this, it needed to be done in a very particular way." The visually stunning show can occasionally require superpowers to track its story lines, but the overall response has been enthusiastic, earning the show a third-season renewal.

Where Marvel goes next, to some degree, is unlimited, given the company's enormous library, including hundreds of obscure heroes and villains. "We tend to do it with the challenge of maybe characters you haven't heard of," Loeb says. "Maybe you don't know who Jessica Jones is; maybe you don't know who the Runaways are. Our hope is we hook you through really strong storytelling, casting and a little bit of luck. And maybe just a sprinkle of magic that you don't ever really want to understand." ☐

CHAPTER 3

CULTURAL

IM

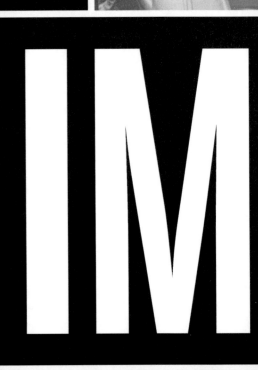

MARVEL HAS LIVED UP TO THE CREDO THAT WITH GREAT POWER COMES GREAT RESPONSIBILITY

PACT

THE BLACK PANTHER PHENOMENON

WAKANDA FOREVER! MARVEL'S FIRST AFRICAN HERO CONQUERED THE BOX OFFICE AND GENERATED UBIQUITOUS CULTURAL INFLUENCE

BY EVAN NARCISSE

FOR THE PAST 11 YEARS, MARVEL STUDIOS' superhero movies have become a hotly anticipated serial saga, a string of global pop-culture events stoking ever higher levels of anticipation and profit. But even for a studio with a record-breaking run of releases, there was nothing like the success of *Black Panther*. In 2018, Wakanda took over the world.

Before *Black Panther* came out, a viral video featuring three friends gushing over a promotional poster racked up millions of views. When New Yorkers Lee Colston, Chris Holland and Clinton Lowe recorded themselves wondering if this is how white people felt all the time, it resonated across the internet. After they saw the movie, Colston said, "The reality is that actually white people don't feel like that all the time because it's so com-

mon for them. They don't have to fight. They're not starved for images in the media that represent their full humanity."

Once it hit theaters, audiences greeted *Black Panther* with a level of enthusiasm and pageantry that happens once in a lifetime. On opening night, moviegoers dressed up in African fashions or their Sunday best for viewing parties, many of them returning to multiplexes several times before the Ryan Coogler–helmed film left theaters. Activist groups set up voter-registration booths at screen-

Scenes from Wakanda (clockwise from top): T'Challa (Chadwick Boseman) and Killmonger (Michael B. Jordan) battle for the throne; Princess Shuri (Letitia Wright) and Queen Ramonda (Angela Bassett); Jabari tribe leader M'Baku (Winston Duke)

ings. Crowdfunding campaigns like marketing consultant Frederick T. Joseph's #BlackPanther-Challenge were launched to make sure under-privileged kids could see the kind of movie that older generations had waited decades for. The film's Los Angeles premiere brought out a who's who of black Hollywood celebrities, including Ava DuVernay, Laurence Fishburne and Don Cheadle. They, too, had been waiting.

A critical hit with seven Oscar nominations (including Best Picture), *Black Panther* was also a massive financial blockbuster, earning $1.3 billion at the worldwide box office.

DESPITE THE FACT that Marvel's superhero movies have become some of the most successful films of all time, *Black Panther* wasn't a guaranteed triumph. When one looks at characters like Captain America and Spider-Man—who have long been top-tier heroes on the comics landscape—it makes sense that they'd be linchpins of film franchises. Black Panther has been a beloved character for decades, but he was a bigger gamble. Until this past year, the king of Wakanda hadn't enjoyed the same kind of awareness and name recognition as his Avengers teammates, and a solo movie seemed like a risk for the Marvel moviemaking machine. But one of the hero's defining characteristics is surprising a world that underestimates him.

Created in 1966 by Stan Lee and Jack Kirby, the Black Panther—also known by his real name, T'Challa—is widely acknowledged as the first black superhero. His debut in *Fantastic Four* No. 52 shows him using an element of surprise that would become his trademark, luring the quartet of science adventurers to his homeland and defeating them in combat. The importance of Wakanda's history also comes through in T'Challa's early adventures, which often noted that the fictional nation had chosen to stay hidden from the outside world to safeguard the super-metal vibranium. Basing a fictional plot point around ultra-rare natural resources deftly alludes to Africa's rancorous real-world relationship with countries from other continents, which took diamonds, coal and—most important—people away to foreign shores for profit. T'Challa's biggest evolutionary leap in comics came during the tenure of writer Christopher Priest, who reimagined the hero in the late 1990s as a Machiavellian master strategist concerned with maintaining Wakanda's sovereignty at all costs. This version of T'Challa, always cognizant of the sacrifices made by his father and other monarchs who preceded him, informed the movie adaptation.

A glorious yet perpetually embattled history was a key factor that award-winning author Ta-Nehisi Coates drew on when he started writing Marvel's main Black Panther comic-book series in 2016. "One of the things I wanted to do is [show] that Wakanda is more than what you see right now," Coates said in interviews at the time. "It's more than the present. Wakanda has history. It's a 3-D place. So when you say you represent a nation as its king or as its queen, you are not just responsible to the citizenry of the present, which T'Challa is answering for. T'Challa is answering for the citizens right now. He's also responsible to that country's history and to everything that came before it."

In both comic books and film, the Black Panther mythos focuses on considerations of power, justice and governance that are rarely tethered to black characters. The movie's central tension revolves around carrying the legacy of the deceased King T'Chaka (T'Challa's father) into an uncertain future. Protected by General Okoye and her elite guard of women warriors called Dora Milaje, T'Challa has to first defeat M'Baku, the leader of the anti-technology Jabari tribe, to become king. Once he ascends to the throne, he must reckon with a Wakanda where different factions disagree about what's best for the country. His biggest threat comes from within his own family. Erik Killmonger is T'Challa's cousin N'Jadaka, abandoned in America after a conflict that led T'Chaka to kill his traitorous brother N'Jobu. He stages a coup to take the throne, in the hopes of using Wakanda's technology and weapons to violently push back against oppression of blacks around the world. T'Challa eventually regains the throne—aided by his genius scientist sister, Shuri, and espionage agent paramour Nakia—and introduces the world to Wakanda at the United Nations.

ONE OF THE elements responsible for *Black Panther*'s record-shattering cinematic performance is the sense of historical import that flowed from

Comic-book writer Ta-Nehisi Coates, left, and film stars Lupita Nyong'o and Chadwick Boseman led fans in a "Wakanda Forever" salute at New York's Apollo Theater.

the movie out into the real world. When Marvel announced plans for the movie in 2014, fans who'd been waiting for the King of Wakanda to show up on the silver screen buzzed with excitement. When T'Challa, played by Chadwick Boseman, was introduced into the Marvel Cinematic Universe in 2016's *Captain America: Civil War*, that buzz grew into a rumble.

Producer Nate Moore wasn't trying to make history when he was championing the project in the halls of Marvel Studios. But he knew that a movie based in Wakanda offered the opportunity to create a revolutionary experience that reflected the African diaspora and black culture. That carried intense pressure. "We were very aware of the legacy of the film industry and how it's treated films about people of color in the past," Moore says. "We were constantly worried. [We thought] if we don't get this right, this could actually make it harder for other films like this to exist."

It was particularly important to the filmmakers that *Black Panther* be acknowledged for its quality and not just because it was a symbolic project. "We

didn't want African and African-American people who saw the film to like it with the caveat 'Well, I mean, it wasn't great, but it was representative, so that's cool,' " Moore admits. "We wanted them to like it because it's a great movie and spoke to an experience that felt authentic."

For his part, Marvel Studios head Kevin Feige had a sense of the unrequited desire for representation that Black Panther fans were harboring. "It's something that's easy to take for granted, growing up in the United States as a white male, that my cinematic heroes look like me," he told Vulture. "I never thought they looked *exactly* like me, because I'm not a big athletic hero, but they do. It's something that over the course of these 10 years, having a certain amount of power over what type of movies are made and what type of actors we hire, I want everybody to have that feeling. We don't take it for granted that people want to see themselves reflected in our heroes and our characters. That's been the case in the comics for years, and, finally, that's the case in the movies, and will only continue from here."

Ryan Coogler has signed on to write and direct a Black Panther *sequel, which could begin production as early as this year.*

THE SHAKESPEAREAN SWEEP of its core conflict made *Black Panther* different from most superhero movies, but it's also unique because the viewer immediately feels how deeply personal the story is. "My whole life I've dealt with issues of identity," director Ryan Coogler told io9.com. "Pretty much ever since my parents sat me down and told me I was black and what that means—which is a strange concept to explain to a child. I couldn't imagine having to do that myself. I don't have kids yet, but it's something that's necessary for you to know. As you get older, you've got to understand who you are and how people see certain conflicts. Or it could cost you your life, frankly."

From Moore and Coogler to production designer Hannah Beachler and costume designer Ruth E. Carter, most of the major decision makers on *Black Panther* came from African-American backgrounds. "When you're talking about building Wakanda and telling this kind of story, that's something that to us just felt narratively true," Moore says. "It was very much Ryan Coogler's intent that the crew should be as diverse as possible." Joe Rob-

ert Cole, who co-wrote the film's screenplay with Coogler, says the production was a group effort in which the cast and crew all strove to create a distinctive superhero movie. The challenge they faced was balancing the demands of telling T'Challa's individual story while also needing to craft something that spoke broadly to the black diasporan experience. "The idea of being able to be a part of bringing forth a hero that was in my image and heritage was something that was very, very special to me," Cole says. "You know your family is going to see it, and there aren't many opportunities to do something on such a large scale."

"I tried to tap into the humanity of my feelings as a member of the African diaspora," he adds. "My confusion, my pride, my fear. I also thought about the roles that women—my grandma and my mom and all my aunties—have played in my life, and trying to present the diversity of thought and ideas in a way where they are multidimensional."

The anticipation surrounding the film led to a wave of creative endeavors beyond Marvel's official moviemaking apparatus. Mechanical engineer

Darian Robbins was just another fan waiting to see Wakanda's king, and long before the character made his onscreen debut in *Captain America: Civil War*, the Maryland native channeled his own excitement into a series of faux magazine covers that created hype for the coming of Prince T'Challa. A multimedia artist in his spare time, Robbins created images that imagined how Wakanda might be covered by magazines like *Wired, Military History Today, Vogue* and—yes—TIME. "Sometimes when you transfer things from one medium to another, things get lost or things get compromised," he said, adding that he wanted to show just how cool Wakanda could be and explaining that his goal with the project was to make "something that people could relate to."

T'CHALLA TAPS INTO the same metaphorical power that Steve Rogers and Tony Stark do. Captain America is a symbol of idealism, and Iron Man represents how cutting-edge technology can radically change our lives, for good or ill. Black Panther is a hero who can simultaneously speak to where black people came from, where they are in the present and where they might go in the future. The beauty of the film is that it creates a fiction that anchors the black diaspora's broken bloodlines in allegorical glory, while still acknowledging the tragedy that disconnected them centuries ago.

Ebony Elizabeth Thomas—an associate professor at the University of Pennsylvania and the author of *The Dark Fantastic: Race and the Imagination from Harry Potter to the Hunger Games*—thinks that *Black Panther* speaks to a deep collective yearning. "For it to defy expectations like it did signals a longing on the part of the body public and seems to signal a longing among audiences to [reckon with and] move on from the white-supremacist past," Thomas theorizes. She also thinks that that same subtext played a part in the character's origins, even if his creators were white. "Kirby and Lee were likely inspired by and responding to black activism at the time," she says. "They were responding directly to the sweeping changes of the civil rights movement."

Moore also says he saw the movie's powerful symbolism extend beyond African-American audiences. "One of my good friends, she has a 11-year-old son," the producer says. "They're a white family, and he went to see *Black Panther* opening weekend.

He came home and was talking about the film and how much he loved it. And when my friend asked, 'Who's your favorite character?', he said General Okoye. And my friend didn't know until she saw the film that his favorite character was an African woman. The film tries to examine representation across not just cultural lines but also gender lines and gender stereotypes. Kids are now embracing heroes and heroines that were not of their own gender, and I think that's really powerful. Frankly, stories like this—that are representative of people who feel underrepresented—have the capacity to reach more people than we give credit for."

CREATING A VISUAL history for a fictional place that would also speak to real-world cultures was a unique challenge. "The real Africa was the inspiration for the Wakandan Africa," says costume designer Carter, a veteran of films like *Malcolm X, Selma* and *Amistad*. For example, "if I saw silver jewelry pieces that were from the [nomadic Saharan tribe] Tuareg, that went into the merchant tribe of Wakanda."

Connections like the ones Carter threaded into the costuming made *Black Panther* the kind of cultural experience that people mark time against, because it feels as if a massive shift of consciousness has happened since the film's release. Before *Black Panther*, there wasn't a contemporary phrase that summed up a collective desire to lash out at racial injustice. Now someone can say "Killmonger was right" and the sentiment they're expressing can instantly be understood. Also, the way that certain lines of dialogue—"I never freeze," "Hey, auntie," "Is this your king?!"—gained traction on social media is a testament to the film's winning formula of familial warmth and dueling philosophies. Simply put, *Black Panther* put on a display of black creativity that defied expectation. "Ryan Coogler and Joe Cole and all of us that worked on *Black Panther* felt like it belonged to every filmmaker, every artist, every activist, every person who said let's try to change the narratives we see about ourselves as black people," says Carter, who notes that she found common cause with the other creators to "bring some beauty and pride to young people." Looking back at the world's embrace of *Black Panther* and the symbolism of Wakanda, she says, "I think the biggest takeaway of it all is that they have their superhero. Finally." □

UNSUNG HEROINES

LIKE THE REST OF THE COMIC-BOOK INDUSTRY, MARVEL HAS HAD A COMPLICATED RELATIONSHIP WITH FEMALE SUPERHEROES OVER THE YEARS

BY LILY ROTHMAN

IT WOULD BE HARD TO NAME THE FIRST FEMALE superhero in American comics history. Contenders include the mystical jungle-protecting Fantomah and the crime-fighting, catsuit-wearing Miss Fury, both of whom debuted before Wonder Woman. So, although it could be easy to think that characters like Captain Marvel and *Black Panther*'s Shuri are an entirely new breed of heroine, they are in fact the daughters of a lineage as old as the comic book itself—and part of a story in which Marvel has played a key part.

"In the very earliest days of comics there were female role models," says Trina Robbins, author of *The Great Women Superheroes* and the artist who in 1970 published the first all-women-produced comic book, *It Ain't Me Babe*. "There were some really cool women characters."

The presence of those women made sense. Super-

hero comics were one component of a world that included many other genres, sold on newsstands. The majority of American kids, boys and girls alike, read comics. With a broad cross section of readers, it was logical that publishers would produce a wide range of characters. In the era of World War II, as women stepped up to help the war effort, so did strong and capable women in the comics.

BUT THE STORY of gender equality in the comics has not been one of steady progress. After all, no matter how supernatural their subjects, comics tend to respond to what's going on in the world that creates them. In the 1950s and '60s, just as real American women often found that the return to postwar normalcy meant a return to domesticity, the women of the comics found their powers reined in. When the

"This book became a sort of victory for the misfits of the world," editor Sana Amanat wrote in the first issue of *Ms. Marvel* in 2014, referring to the initial announcement that the series was coming. The book starred Muslim American teenager Kamala Khan, who is transformed into the titular superhero and can stretch, enlarge or shrink her arms, legs and body.

Director Anna Boden worked with actors Jude Law and Lee Pace on the set of Captain Marvel, *the 21st film in the Marvel Cinematic Universe.*

Comics Magazine Association of America tried to curtail criticism by regulating the medium's morals, the resulting 1954 code reinforced that trend, clarifying an industry interest in "the value of the home and the sanctity of marriage."

For Hope Nicholson, author of *The Spectacular Sisterhood of Superwomen*, one particular Marvel superheroine illustrates this idea: Invisible Girl. She was a historic character—the first female superhero of the so-called Silver Age from the company—introduced by Stan Lee and Jack Kirby in *The Fantastic Four* No. 1 in 1961. But while she broke a glass ceiling, she didn't always break the mold. Her actions were often driven by domestic and familial concerns. She was an adult from the get-go, but her name wouldn't become "Invisible Woman" until 1985. (Meanwhile, though a teen, Spider-Man was never Spider-Boy.) She was just one woman on a team of men. (This situation mirrored what was happening behind the scenes; in this period, Marvel artist Marie Severin stood out in a male-dominated field.) Invisible Girl also, of course, had a tendency to disappear.

"There are female superheroes who challenge this dominant cultural narrative of women being weak, but on the other hand they're a very small number and they're pretty much all stereotypes," says Carolyn Cocca, author of *Superwomen: Gender, Power, and Representation.*

By the 1970s and early '80s, the idea of women's liberation was beginning to be better understood by a wider swath of society and more female superheroes were appearing. Just look at what happened to Carol Danvers: introduced in 1968 in a minor part, in 1977 she gained an expanded role and an overtly feminist name, Ms. Marvel.

The Cat, arriving in 1972, made explicit mention of women's lib and was written by a woman, Linda Fite (with Severin drawing the book). The powerful Storm, introduced in 1975, would appear among the X-Men, the Fantastic Four and the Avengers, as well as marrying Black Panther. She-Hulk, who debuted in 1980, was a New York City lawyer in her day job. Kitty Pryde, introduced in 1980, started out timid but grew in power within the X-Men universe, and original X-Men member Jean Grey did too. Monica Rambeau, a black woman, brought ethnic diversity into the Captain Marvel character in 1982. You didn't have to be a superfan to see what was happening. A 1978 *Newsweek* headline blared the takeaway: "Superwomen Fight Back!"

Once again, however, the progress toward gender equality among superheroes did not continue uninterrupted. In 1989, the Comics Code dropped the requirement that female bodies be depicted realistically. Combine that change with the rise of bodybuilding and the mainstreaming of pornography, Cocca says, and you end up with a notable sexualizing of the superheroine. The comics economy was changing too. Books were increasingly purchased in specialty stores—a situation that could, experts believe, foster a sense of exclusivity among those who supposedly "belonged" at a comics shop. Without the need to appeal to the newsstand audience, producers often narrowed their offerings to those designed to appeal to that particular, often male, crowd.

That didn't mean readers stopped wanting female superheroes—and wanting them to be as well-rounded, interesting and smart as their more numerous male counterparts. Meanwhile, the format itself was evolving. Trina Robbins credits the 1980 graphic novel *Maus* and the popularity of the Japanese manga series *Sailor Moon* in the 1990s with showing the world what comics could be. Especially in indie comics, the number of women working behind the scenes increased. And the rise of fan conventions and the internet allowed fans of all kinds to speak to creators. Though Cocca and Nicholson both acknowledge that some fans would prefer to keep the comics just the way they were in the past, many others used that access to ask for change.

BEFORE LONG, THE result could be seen on the page and screen. In 2015, when Marvel launched its "All-New, All-Different" branding, it included more than a dozen female-led titles, a major uptick. "It's so energizing to people who have felt left out from the superhero universe," Cocca says. The results in the Marvel Universe include brand-new characters as well as new identities for old ones (and often with female writers and artists working on the titles).

Spider-Woman became a single mom in a recent reboot. Thor's sister Angela was introduced in 2014; a woman has also picked up Thor's own hammer and assumed the role of the goddess of thunder.

The new Ms. Marvel is Kamala Khan, a Muslim teenager. The all-female A-Force team was introduced in 2015. As of 2014, the New Avengers team has filled the role of Dr. Spectrum, a scientist, with a woman. The Young Avengers include America Chavez, a gay Latinx woman. Jumping off the page, Netflix's *Jessica Jones* offers a female superhero who's gritty and realistic, while *Black Panther*'s Shuri presented a woman of fantastical smarts and wit. The Disney Channel animated series *Marvel Rising* features several young female heroes at the forefront. And that's just a small sample. Things have changed behind the scenes too. With *Guardians of the Galaxy*, Nicole Perlman became the first woman to be credited as a writer on a Marvel movie. "I do still feel like it's a little bit like, 'Wow, it's so crazy that a woman is doing this!' I look forward to the time when it won't be that crazy," she told TIME in 2014.

Which is not to say that this story is over. As beloved as many of the new characters may be, your default superhero is still likely to be male. Cocca's research indicates that, among superhero TV shows airing that season or in development as of early 2019, about 10% star women. The ratio is about the same in comics, and it's only 15% in the movies. Other research backs up her findings. A study by journalist Amanda Shendruk found in 2017 that about a quarter of Marvel and DC characters were women but that fewer than half that ratio of major superhero comics were female-led, and that even fewer mixed-gender teams had more women than men. Among the current female writers working for Marvel are Gail Simone (*Domino*), Kelly Thompson (*Captain Marvel* and *West Coast Avengers*), Vita Ayala (*Shuri*), Jen and Sylvia Soska (*Black Widow*), Rainbow Rowell (*Runaways*), Mariko Tamaki (*X-23*) and Nilah Magruder (*Marvel Rising*).

Having experienced firsthand this pendulum of representation, Robbins is optimistic. Marvel's new female characters, she says, are "terrific." Once again, larger societal changes have led to changes in the world of superheroes. As women across the country and world have found solidarity in voicing their concerns and experiences, women who want to see themselves as super can do so too. The world is listening. "There are people of all sorts speaking up and saying, 'I don't see anyone on the pages of the comics that reminds me of me,'" Robbins says. "When I was a voice in the wilderness, I never even dreamed it would get this good." □

EARTH'S MIGHTIEST POP-CULTURE INFLUENCE

THE MARVEL HEROES ARE FREQUENT FODDER FOR ENTERTAINMENT PARODIES

▷ **Homer Simpson "Hulked out"** after falling into a pool of green paint in a 2002 episode of *The Simpsons*.

△ **The stars of the Marvel Cinematic Universe** have been popular guests on late-night television, including this 2015 visit to *Jimmy Kimmel Live!* to play "Avengers Family Feud."

△ **In a 2005 episode of *The O.C.*,** Seth and Summer paid homage to the classic kiss from the first *Spider-Man* movie.

◁ **The cast of *black-ish*** celebrated Halloween last year with *Black Panther*–themed costumes.

△ ***Sesame Street* has featured several Marvel parodies,** including two different takes on the Fantastic Four. "The Furry Four" (above) aired in 2010, and "The Fantabulous Four" followed in 2014.

The rapper Ghostface Killah is a huge Iron Man fan—he uses the alias "Tony Starks"—and his song "Slept on Tony" was featured in *Iron Man*.

Disney Channel cartoon stars Phineas and Ferb met the Avengers in the 2013 crossover special "Mission Marvel." Stan Lee also appeared, as a hot dog vendor.

Live from New York...
SNL Loves Marvel

Over the years, *Saturday Night Live* has enjoyed poking fun at the Marvel universe. Clockwise from top: in a 2018 Black Panther sketch, T'Challa is reunited with his loud, less-than-regal Uncle M'Butu (Kenan Thompson) in the spiritual plane; Andrew Garfield and his *Amazing Spider-Man* co-star Emma Stone share a series of sloppy and awkward kisses in 2014; a mock trailer for a Black Widow solo film finds Scarlett Johansson juggling romance and a magazine internship in 2015; that same year, the Avengers celebrate their victory over Ultron in a local news report in which they announce plans for a victory party at a Dave & Busters, complete with karaoke; and Kirsten Dunst gets hit on by on a too-friendly neighborhood Spider-Man in her 2002 opening monologue.

SUPER-POWERED PROFITS

FROM VIDEO GAMES TO JELL-O, HIGHLIGHTS OF MARVEL'S BUSINESS EMPIRE

One of the tastier tie-ins to last year's *Avengers: Infinity War* was a colorful assortment of special Jell-O packaging.

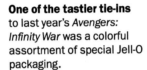

Marvel characters have been immortalized as part of the cult-favorite Funko Pop vinyl-figure line.

Shoppers in a Parisian toy store perused an assortment of toys, action figures and costumes.

Marvel's Spider-Man was one of the most popular video games of 2018, selling more than 5 million copies.

The Avengers have assembled on baseball caps, T-shirts, jackets, pajamas, socks, sneakers and, of course, Halloween costumes.

The Incredible Hulk Coaster is a popular ride at Universal's Islands of Adventure park in Orlando, Fla. (above). Among the Disney California Adventure Park attractions in Anaheim is a Guardians of the Galaxy ride.

The popularity of Marvel movies has given a big boost to toy company Hasbro. Marvel is ranked as one of the top five toy brands in the U.S.

TIME

Editor Edward Felsenthal
Creative Director D.W. Pine

The World of Marvel

Editorial Director Kostya Kennedy
Editor Rich Sands
Designer Martin Gee
Photo Editor Liz Ronk
Writers John Anderson, Bob Batchelor, Anthony Breznican, Richard Corliss, Eliana Dockterman, Lev Grossman, Emily Joshu, Courtney Mifsud, Evan Narcisse, Marisa Roffman, Lily Rothman, Richard Schickel, Stephanie Zacharek
Copy Editor Joseph McCombs
Researcher Tresa McBee
Production Designer Jennifer Panzer
Editorial Production David Sloan

MEREDITH SPECIAL INTEREST MEDIA
Senior Vice President, Finance Anthony Palumbo
Vice President, Marketing Jeremy Biloon
Director, Brand Marketing Jean Kennedy
Sales Director Christi Crowley
Associate Director, Brand Marketing Bryan Christian
Associate Director, Finance Jill Earyes
Senior Brand Manager Katherine Barnet

Editorial Director Kostya Kennedy
Creative Director Gary Stewart
Director of Photography Christina Lieberman
Editorial Operations Director Jamie Roth Major
Manager, Editorial Operations Gina Scauzillo
Special thanks: Don Armstrong, Brad Beatson, Helen Eisenbach, Melissa Frankenberry, Kate Roncinske

MEREDITH NATIONAL MEDIA GROUP
President Jon Werther
Meredith Magazines President Doug Olson
President, Meredith Digital Stan Pavlovsky
President, Consumer Products Tom Witschi
Chief Revenue Officer Michael Brownstein
Chief Marketing & Data Officer Alysia Borsa
Marketing & Integrated Communications Nancy Weber

SENIOR VICE PRESIDENTS
Consumer Revenue Andy Wilson
Digital Sales Marla Newman
Research Solutions Britta Cleveland
Product & Technology Justin Law
Chief Digital Officer Matt Minoff
Corporate Sales Brian Kightlinger

VICE PRESIDENTS
Finance Chris Susil
Business Planning & Analysis Rob Silverstone
Direct Media Patti Follo
Strategic Sourcing, Newsstand, Production Chuck Howell
Consumer Marketing Steve Crowe
Brand Licensing Steve Grune

Vice President, Group Editorial Director Stephen Orr
Director, Editorial Operations & Finance Greg Kayko

MEREDITH CORPORATION
President & Chief Executive Officer Tom Harty
Chief Financial Officer Joseph Ceryanec
Chief Development Officer John Zieser
President, Meredith Local Media Group Patrick McCreery
Senior Vice President, Human Resources Dina Nathanson

Executive Chairman Stephen M. Lacy
Vice Chairman Mell Meredith Frazier

Credits

Cover
© Marvel Studios, 2018

Back Cover
Josef Kubes/Alamy

Title
1 David Pokress/Newsday via Getty Images

Table of Contents
2–3 Laura Cavanaugh/FilmMagic/Getty Images

Chapter 1
5 Fantastic Four #1 (artist: Jack Kirby), © Marvel **6** Jonathan Leibson/Getty Images for Samsung **8–9** Classic Image/Alamy **11** Josef Kubes/Alamy **12–13** William Sauro/The New York Times/Redux **14** Shutterstock **17** Susan Skaar/Creative Commons **19** Amazing Spider-Man #33 (artist: Steve Ditko), © Marvel **21** Evan Hurd/Corbis via Getty Images **22–23** (clockwise from top left) Columbia/Kobal/Shutterstock; Kerry Hayes/20th Century Fox/Kobal/Shutterstock; Cliff Lipson/CBS via Getty Images; Richard Cartwright/ABC via Getty Images; Fox via Getty Images **24** (from top) X-Men #1 (artist: Jack Kirby), © Marvel; Incredible Hulk #181 (artist: Herb Trimpe), © Marvel **25** Captain America Comics #1 (artist: Jack Kirby), © Marvel **26** The Uncanny X-Men #135 (artist: John Byrne), © Marvel **27** Amazing Spider-Man #33 (artist: Steve Ditko), © Marvel **28** Captain Marvel #1 (artist: Ed McGuinness), © Marvel **29** Black Panther #1 (artist: Brian Stelfreeze), © Marvel

Chapter 2
30 (clockwise from top left) © Marvel Studios; Marvel/Paramount/Kobal/Shutterstock; Chuck Zlotnick/© Marvel Studios; Zade Rosenthal/© Marvel Studios; Chuck Zlotnick/© Marvel Studios; © Marvel Studios **31** (clockwise from top left) © Marvel Studios; Zade Rosenthal/© Marvel Studios; © Marvel Studios (2); Ben Rothstein/© Marvel Studios; Chuck Zlotnick/© Marvel Studios **33** Denise Truscello/Getty Images Portrait **37** Chuck Zlotnick/© Marvel Studios **38** Chuck Zlotnick/© Marvel Studios **41** (clockwise from left) Marvel/Walt Disney Pictures/Kobal/Shutterstock; Matt Kennedy/© Marvel Studios; Chuck Zlotnick/Columbia/Kobal/Shutterstock **42** Yasuyoshi Chiba/AFP/Getty Images **45** Zade Rosenthal/© Marvel Studios **46** Marvel Enterprises/Kobal/Shutterstock **47** (from top) Francois Duhamel/© Marvel Studios; Marvel/Paramount/Kobal/Shutterstock **48** (from left) Zade Rosenthal/© Marvel Studios; Mark Fellman/© Marvel Studios **49** Marvel/Paramount/Kobal/Shutterstock **50** © Marvel Studios **51** (from top) Zade Rosenthal/© Marvel Studios; © Marvel Studios **52** (from top) Jay Maidment/© Marvel Studios; © Marvel Studios **53** (from top) © Marvel Studios; Zade Rosenthal/© Marvel Studios **54–57** © Marvel Studios **58** Jay Maidment/© Marvel Studios **59** (from top) © Marvel Studios; Chuck Zlotnick/© Marvel Studios **60** Chuck Zlotnick/Columbia/Kobal/Shutterstock **61** © Marvel Studios (2) **62** © Marvel Studios (2) **63** (from top) © Marvel Studios; Chuck Zlotnick/© Marvel Studios **64** (from top) Ben Rothstein/© Marvel Studios; © Marvel Studios **65** © Marvel Studios **67** (clockwise from top left) Attila Dory/20th Century Fox/Marvel Ent Group/Kobal/Shutterstock; 20th Century Fox/Marvel/Kobal/Shutterstock; Moviestore Collection/Shutterstock **68** Marvel Enterprises/20th Century Fox/Kobal/Shutterstock **70–71** © Columbia Pictures/courtesy Everett Collection **73** CBS via Getty Images **74–75** (from left) ABC/Photofest; © Fox Kids Network/Photofest; Jennifer Clasen/ABC via Getty Images **76–77** (from left) Moviestore Collection/Shutterstock; David Giesbrecht/Netflix; Suzanne Tenner/© FX/courtesy Everett Collection

Chapter 3
78–79 (clockwise from top left) Ollie Millington/Getty Images; Roger Kisby/Redux; David Maung/EPA-EFE/Shutterstock; Daniel Knighton/FilmMagic/Getty Images; Roger Kisby/Redux **81** (clockwise from top left) Matt Kennedy/© Marvel Studios (2); © Marvel Studios **83** Shahar Azran/WireImage/Getty Images **84** Bill O'Leary/The Washington Post via Getty Images **87** Ms. Marvel #1 (artist: Sara Pichelli), © Marvel **88** © Marvel Studios **90** (from top) © Fox/Photofest; Randy Holmes/ABC via Getty Images **91** (clockwise from top left) ABC via Getty Images; © WB/Courtesy Everett Collection; Richard Termine/Sesame Street **92** (from top) Mark Horton/Getty Images; Disney XD via Getty Images **93** (from top) Will Heath/NBC/NBCU Photo Bank via Getty Images; Dana Edelson/NBC/Getty Images (4) **94** (clockwise from top right) Pascal Sittler/REA/Redux; Courtesy Playstation; Carolyn Jenkins/Alamy; Mim Friday/Alamy; Pisit Khambubpha/Alamy; Courtesy Kraft Heinz; Jennifer Star/Alamy

Last Word
96 Martin Schoeller/August

'NUFF SAID

"Stan Lee created a universe where, if a character was beloved enough, they could never really die. Now *that's* thinking ahead."
—THE AVENGERS DIRECTOR JOSS WHEDON, PAYING TRIBUTE TO LEE, NOVEMBER 2018

Made in the USA
Middletown, DE
17 April 2019